Reflections of a
CHAMPION

Gary Lee Brown

PAGE PUBLISHING
Conneaut Lake, PA

First originally published by Page Publishing 2022

ISBN 978-1-6624-7856-7 (pbk)
ISBN 979-8-88654-696-5 (hc)
ISBN 978-1-6624-7858-1 (digital)

Printed in the United States of America

CONTENTS

★ 1971: Born - June 25th on Amityville, Long Island

★ 1989: Graduated from Brentwood Highschool

★ 1989 - 1992: Began NCAA football career at Nassau
Community College
  ○ Voted All American by NCAA as a senior.

★ 1992 - 1993: Transferred to Georgia Tech

★ 1994: Drafted by the Pittsburgh Steelers in the 5th
round, draft pick 148

★ 1994: Acquired by Green Bay Packers

★ 1997: Won Super Bowl 31 with the Green Bay Packers

★ 1998 - 2003: Played with the San Francisco 49ers -
Barcelona Dragons - CFL Hamilton Tiger Cats

★ 2009: Work injury leads to paralysis

★ 2011: Serious life change needed - Signed up for Big
Brothers Big Sisters and began philanthropic work

★ 2015: Founded Dream68 - focused on serving
underprivileged youth across the country

★ Today: Empowering others to overcome any obstacle
through positivity and giving back

ACKNOWLEDGMENTS

I would like to start by thanking the reader for listening to my story with an open mind and sincere heart.

I would like to thank my parents, who gave me all the tools and direction through love and guidance to get me to this point in my life.

Thank you to everyone mentioned in this book who has played an important role in the choices I have made and to the many others not mentioned in this book.

Thank you to David Lionheart, who helped bring my story to life for others to enjoy, learn, and teach from.

Thank you to my family, who has stood by me and dealt with all the late-night tears of joy and pain that came with honestly retelling these stories.

I thank *God* for giving me the strength, courage, and opportunity not only to live and survive this story but for the awareness to understand that it could help someone someplace at some time.

Thank you, thank you, thank you. Enjoy!

Introduction by
David Lionheart

In *Reflections of a Champion*, we discuss the inspiring journey Gary has been on and continues to forge. The book covers his climb from youth football in Brentwood, New York, to a Super Bowl championship in Green Bay, Wisconsin.

Gary narrowly escapes the evil call of the streets while barely holding on to his dreams. He reveals his struggles when dealing with social injustice, fame, depression, and the aftermath of his career-ending injuries.

Gary bravely talks through becoming paralyzed and his continuous uphill battle to walk again. An unexpected overdose turns into a blessing in helping Gary establish a new life after pro sports. We discover the positive impact that philanthropy has had on Gary's recovery physically, mentally, and emotionally. He shares more than a sports story with the world. He shares his heart and soul in a vulnerable way so that others who can relate may choose to live.

INTRODUCTION

I moved my weathered elbows forward one at a time, pinning them to the floor like ice picks penetrating a steep mountain face. Toxic sweat ran freely from my throbbing forehead. I was cursing and praying while pulling my upper body in a rhythmic pace to guide my stomach across the filthy bedroom floor. The torturous journey seemed like miles. Completely exhausted, I dragged my lifeless legs as a tractor would while pulling two rusty sickles through stiff dirt. Reality had set in.

I was at home and almost four hundred pounds. I was paralyzed and needed to go to the bathroom. Who else was going to get me there? To think I may never walk again and that this was what life was going to look like was very depressing, almost life-threatening. I was panting, crying, and begging to know "Why me!" How the hell did I get here?

Chapter 1

LOOK AT THE SIZE OF THOSE MITTS

Mr. John stood out on the field that day, watching the shoulder pads smack against one another as players moved from drill to drill. I had been playing quarterback leading up to middle school, and on that day, that was going to change.

Coach John was a large-framed man. He stood watching over the field like a stadium light as the players tackled one another. He was an athlete himself, and I recall him moving well for a larger man.

That year, I was expecting to continue as quarterback, but Mr. John quickly corrected me. I can remember standing there as he held my hands in between us with the palms facing the sky.

"Look at the size of those mitts!" he exclaimed.

He was our head coach, and a damn good one at that. He saw something in me that would go on to change my career and ultimately my life.

"We are going to teach you how to block and how to use your feet and then find you a position that you can grow into," he softly preached.

This can be a little intimidating for a child who could just as easily stick to what they knew. It was a good lesson for me in adaptation and trust. Stepping out of our comfort zones is never a bad thing.

He moved me to different offensive positions like wide receiver and tight end. He put me with the offensive lineman, exposing me to blocking, and then eventually to the defensive line to complete the learning experience. At times, I missed playing quarterback and was a little heartbroken. However, I trusted him and bought into the process. He was a good man, and I knew he wouldn't steer me wrong.

What Mr. John was doing for me was more than I understood. For this book, I interviewed him. He is now in his seventies. It was so awesome to walk down memory lane with him as he recalled one specific quality I had that no one else had. He joyfully shared, "I can't remember what I had for dinner last night, but I remember Gary Brown running around that field, trying harder than anyone else." No matter what he asked me to do or where he told me to go, I did it. I never asked questions or went against his grain. I believed in him because he believed in me.

A good coach can elevate someone beyond their own understood potential. Hard work and tough love can be dealt with without hurting the athlete's opportunity or experience. A coach trying to relive moments of their own careers that never came to fruition can force a young kid away. When they get forced away from sports, there is a good chance that you won't get them back.

I was fifteen years old and finishing up my freshman year. Mr. John gave me the team's White Letter Award. This was the award every player wanted to get. It did not just focus on your sports accomplishments. Instead, it complimented your character as a teammate and student. It praised someone who was where they were told to be, someone who did what they were asked to do, and above all, someone who led by example. Mr. John said it was an easy decision as I stood out to him in so many ways. On the field, I was excelling in all my new positions or at least willing to try. Off the field, he helped me become a leader and praised me for my personal character. It was the perfect balance for a young athlete.

Mr. John saw something in me at a young age. By introducing me to those drills and expectations, it put me on track to become an exceptional offensive lineman. I would play this position at Nassau Community College, Georgia Tech, and in the NFL.

I never took steroids or other performance-enhancing drugs (aka PEDs). I never cheated in the game. I worked harder than the guy across from me on every play. No matter what, I gave my coaches and my team everything I had in me. I also made sure I was doing my part off the field in supporting my peers.

Kids are fragile. They carry so much weight on their shoulders and oftentimes need that positive guidance. When they are part of a team, they look to the coach for that reinforcement and trust. The coach has to be a stronger and more reliable voice than the voices calling these kids into a life of crime or misconduct. No matter where you come from, kids listen to the evil voices that call. These voices can lead to self-harm, crime, and separation from parental guidance. If a kid is not at practice, where do you think they are going to go?

Parents are just as influential on a kid's sports development. It can lead to disaster when you have angry parents interfering in practices, yelling at refs during games, and putting unnecessary pressure on the kids to win. When did winning become bigger than the children learning true sportsmanship? What do you think these kids will do when they grow up and have kids of their own?

It's a chain reaction started by negative leaders put in front of our kids that can have damaging effects on them for the rest of their lives. When you show your kids an example of lacking respect, they will mimic it just as you have. We need to help them become strong, positive, compassionate, and understanding leaders.

It is an understatement that sports has a huge influence in our world. It does more than bring value to the school's identity. More importantly, it brings value to the child's identity. For that young person to be accountable and accepted in a positive group or situation can be a matter of life and death. They are not just numbers, they are people that will go on to live their own lives.

I was heavily influenced by Mr. John in such a positive way. He would go on to coach thousands of kids in his career. At the end of my interview with him, I asked him what his greatest coaching moment was. With a chuckle, he let me know, "It was you winning the Super Bowl. I think I have told everyone I know about it. I have the ball you sent me with the photos signed at my house to this day. Even though all my grandkids want it, I will never give it up. It means so much to me."

Humbled, I let him know I would never have made it there if it wasn't for him connecting with me, believing in me, and helping me learn. I told him how much I respected him for that back then and even more so today.

At the end of our talk, I informed him that after football, I suffered an injury and was paralyzed from the waist down. At first, silent and obviously concerned, he asked what I did about it. I told him how I tackled one day at a time, one moment at a time, and one step at a time. I cried one tear at a time and grinded out one therapy session at a time until finally, I was able to walk again.

I could feel his heart swell over the phone. He softly murmured, "Of course, that's what you did, Gary, because that is exactly who you are. You are the hardest worker, and you never quit." We both were on the verge of tears as we parted from the phone call. He might not know it, but he helped me learn to think that way because of the way he coached me. These important moments enriched my childhood and helped build my football legacy.

Every child that I work with receives a piece of what Mr. John did for me. I want them to continue to play and understand the power of a positive relationship on their sports teams. My hope is that they go on to contribute to our society in a safe and positive way as friends, parents, and maybe even coaches themselves.

Chapter 2

Coaching 101: We Could Be Heroes

I have amazing parents who were very involved in our lives. We were raised differently in my house. As a blue-collar, hardworking family, Mom and Dad always made sure we had what we needed and some of what we wanted.

They both were constantly navigating through life's many challenges with a positive attitude. Through all the ups and downs, they stayed married and in love. A lot of my friends came from broken homes, so whenever they came to visit, it was nice for them to be able to experience the love, structure, and care that comes from a household like the one I grew up in. My parents were parents for the neighborhood.

My mother was a nurse, and anyone on the block who was hurt came to her for help. She saw everything from cuts to bruises to pimples and fixed them all. You could always tell if someone was really hurt or if they wanted to see what she was cooking that day.

My father was the commissioner of youth sports in Brentwood. He and his coaches were a major influence on a lot of kids who lived in our area. As an athlete himself, he understood the power of sports and how it can save the lives of kids. He would pay their way if they needed the registration fee, and he would make sure everyone who needed a ride had it.

He was big on accountability. Dad was always checking in with all the players on his teams, reminding them to be at practice on time and following it with "Don't forget your sneakers!" Children really need that.

As kids, all we had was one another out there, running around, playing kick the can and tag, and doing whatever we could to stay busy while making do with our personalities and imaginations.

There was also a certain kind of freedom that came with that lifestyle we grew up with. Our parents trusted us. We did all our chores, worked around the house, and then were sent out to play. From daybreak to dinnertime, we were always out having fun. No toys, just each other.

One summer, we even started collecting bike parts from all over to be able to make one another bikes. Once we got enough parts to fix a bike for one of us to ride, we then moved on to the next one, one piece at a time. These bonds that we formed together carried over into our school and travel sports. And of course, my father was at the root of that tree.

You have to understand that while we were lucky to have my parents, there were kids whose parents were not around. Oftentimes those parents worked multiple jobs or were in negative spaces themselves. Eventually, absent parents lose control. The parents that are trapped in what life dealt them directly impact their children.

Oftentimes there were little to no options for kids, leading them to hanging out with the wrong crowd. If you lose your young ones to the streets at that early age, you may never get them back. They need guidance, positivity, and stability. Here is where good parenting becomes good coaching. Here is how sports or a group activity can save a kid's life.

My parents prepared us to be coached at an early age. We had that trust with them, and they were always there for us. Even when my father wasn't coaching me, he and my mother were constantly making sure we grew up around a positive structure. Taking responsibility for ourselves and being accountable for our actions were part of our upbringing.

At an early age, we were doing all kinds of chores, and let me tell you, I could make a bed just as well as any turndown service. I remember doing everything from braiding my sister's hair to helping dad with house projects while maintaining our studies.

I can recall sitting at my kitchen table, trying to grind through my schoolwork, which did not come easy for me. Even though I could see all the kids playing outside already, my mother sat there and made sure I finished all my work.

I was a struggling *C* student, meaning I had to try so hard just to get the *C*. I wasn't lazy; I just couldn't pay attention. My mother worked so hard to help me and my siblings succeed academically.

She would get off work, do all her house chores, and then carve out the time for our schoolwork. Once we were in bed, she would stay up and do her homework for the degree she was working toward. Whenever someone says they don't have time to do something, I think about her. There were never any excuses, she just did it.

All these actions helped lead up to my opportunity to play sports and be part of a team. I would get the chance to stand behind the whistle instead of having it blown at me. The experience would go on to be one of the greatest sports moments of my career.

After our senior year in high school, my father was in charge of the youth basketball league. A coach decided to quit, leaving a vacancy that needed to be filled, or else the kids would not be able to play. My father asked me and my long-time friend Kevin to take on the job, and we happily accepted. We did not really understand what we were getting into until the first day of practice.

The reason this team was so unique revealed itself on opening night. The sound of sneakers squeaking and streaking on the shiny floor echoed in the gym. Like clockwork, eight groups of kids moved from drill to drill, showcasing their abilities. Nervously and clumsily performing the tasks at each station, each kid was hoping they would be part of the winning team when all was said and done.

Once the drills were conducted, all the coaches went behind closed doors and chose their players for that year's league. This was when Dad found out that the last coach did not show up to draft. As a result, the other teams were able to have the top choice of all the kids who stood out during the exercises. The kids that were left over ended up on the same team. That team was now ours.

Kevin and I would become strongly connected in our own sports careers. We have been friends since elementary school, and we were part of the same crew growing up. We would go on to play varsity basketball together, and he was a great player.

He was definitely better at basketball than me and would go on to play for Nassau Community College. I would go on to play football at the same school. It's cool that two childhood friends now found themselves at the helm of a coaching job for a misfit team that my father donned on us.

Our "Bad News Bears" team looked like this. We had three girls including my sister, one heavyset girl who did not want to be there because her parents were forcing her to be there to lose some weight, and a kid who thought he was Michael Jordan and did everything we told him not to do. He wanted to do the fancy footwork and none of the gritty teamwork.

With a late registration, we were also granted a young kid named Matt. He would go on to be our best player and a positive glue to keep all the kids focused while playing together. Matt could fill in the blanks whenever we needed him too. He was there when our team needed a score, an assist, or to make a big defensive stop.

We kept the atmosphere lighthearted and productive. It was more important that we got them to fall in love with being there rather than turning them into Hall of Famers in our first season.

We tried getting them used to moving around and doing it as a team. The only thing worse than a coach who doesn't show up to pick their team is one who shows up and tries to live unfulfilled dreams through the experiences of the children that they are coaching.

The other coaches were almost militant in style. There was screaming, yelling, and hard discipline blaring from the other side-lines. They had to run laps and do push-ups for missing shots or dropping balls. *The kids are so young,* I thought. It made me so sad to see them going through that experience. The coaches were taking all the genuine fun out of the sport for them.

When one of our kids made an error, we carefully corrected them. More importantly, we made sure we put them on a pedestal when they did something right. We focused on stringing together positive experiences and small victories in order to accomplish the big win when we needed it most.

The season was a mixed bag. Every team we played against was like going up against the power of the New York Yankees. Sometimes we would only score a couple of points, and they would use the mercy rule on us. Other times we would somehow squeak out a win. We kept it fun still, even during those games that were blowouts.

We often created mini competitions among ourselves that had nothing to do with the actual game. We told them not to look at the scoreboard but instead focus on hitting our internal goals, which we set in order to make the games fun. The parents and other teams were probably scratching their heads as to why our kids were happy and high-fiving even during a blowout loss.

Our team managed to string a couple of wins together as the season went on. We made it through the playoffs and miraculously found ourselves in the championship game.

These were not the same kids who were swept under the rug on draft night. They had a season to build their confidence and have fun playing the game. Most importantly, they became united as a team.

We found ways to celebrate and praise them even if it was not basketball related. "One basket, one stop, and one moment at a time" was our motto. Staying the course, we put up a fight for the coveted championship.

The big moments started coming. Our players were taking turns inking pages in our soon-to-be epic story. This heavyset girl hit her first basket of the season, turned to the crowd, and shrieked with joy, "Mom, I did it!" It was awesome!

The kid who thought he was MJ came up big, hitting a 3-pointer with an extra-point foul shot to give us a boost. Matt played his heart out, diving for loose balls, assisting his teammates, and hitting crucial buckets.

We did it. Our team put together enough plays, enough baskets, and enough defensive stops together to beat our opponent. We did everything we could to win the game. Somehow we won, and most importantly, we had fun doing it.

As the championship win started sinking in for the kids, there were tears, cheers, and celebrations. You would have thought we won the NBA finals. Across the court, the other coach was having the kids run punishment laps.

The losing team circled the gym and our smiling faces as they were being yelled at for failing to win. The image of that was enough to get our point across on how important it is for coaches to keep the game fun for the kids.

We were not even out of the gym yet, and we were being swarmed by other parents asking if their kids could play on our team next year. It wouldn't stop there. For the next month, my father was getting letters from parents requesting their kids play for us the following season. They saw what we did, with who we did it, and how we made sure the game was made fun.

We wished we could have coached again, but we were both off to Nassau Community College to start our own respective seasons. Kevin was playing basketball for them, and I was playing football. If football did not work out for me, I really wanted to coach. Thankfully, I coached them for the one season. I will surely never forget those kids.

One of the coolest parts of that season was that my sister was on that same team. She ended up getting a scholarship to play basketball and is now a teacher herself. I am so proud of her and glad to have even a small part in her story.

Good coaching can change a kid's life while bad coaching can ruin a child's perceptions of sports for life. Looking back at my career, I can remember all the special men and women who made a difference for me in my path to playing football. I'm so thankful to them all.

Chapter 3

I'm Gonna Make You Quit

In tenth grade, I was more preoccupied with hanging out or chasing love than starting at quarterback. The coaches always had a bitter taste in their mouth from that.

They felt strongly that I could have contributed to the team winning. At the high school level, every kid who was even moderately athletic mattered and was greatly needed. To think about it from the student's standpoint, time is short. You only get four years of high school sports, so to miss out on any of that time for any reason can be costly. It is time you can never get back.

It's incredible to think of the student athletes who really take advantage of that opportunity and make the most of it. They will have those skill sets and memories forever.

When I finally decided to commit to playing high school football, my head coach welcomed me back to tryouts by telling me exactly how it was going to be: "I'm not gonna cut you. I'm gonna make you quit." That was exactly what he tried to do.

Coach would have my teammates doing three sprints and make me do four. He would have them do twenty push-ups and then have me do thirty. He was laser-focused on making me miserable, or was trying to anyway.

I can still hear his voice stampeding through my helmet, saying, "Brown, you're never going to make it on this team. You might as well get out of here now." The other kids did not really know who

I was, so I decided to stay focused and follow the crowd to the next drill. They were probably happy he was all over me and not them.

This was a big turning point for me in my personal growth. If I became prideful and walked off the field, then I would have never learned what was really happening. I would have grown up thinking that coach was just a jerk, blaming him for my quitting football.

On the outside, he treated me harshly and purposefully. He did so by giving me all those extra reps to do and continuously singling me out in front of everyone on a pressure-filled stage to perform. I know somewhere inside him as a coach, he had to respect my determination. That's what you want in a young player and, more importantly, a young man.

The extra coaching and attention led to my understanding that I could overcome anything in front of me. I was not going to be the guy that stopped and quit. If all I had to do was outlast everyone else, then I vowed to be the last man standing no matter what. I was now ready to give it my all on the field.

I continued to grow that year physically and mentally. My high school football career was exceptional. I was able to play several positions really well, all while developing my football IQ. Hard work, determination, and a strong love for the game would prepare me to play at the next level. Everything I learned along the way would be needed to overcome the next series of challenges I would go on to face.

I was hoping to start my football career as a freshman at Nassau Community College. My body was strong and in great football shape, but there was such a huge pool of motivated talent standing in my way. I worked really hard at adjusting to the next level of physical demands as well as the psychological pressures of college football.

After the grueling tryouts, we all slowly shuffled over to the coaches' office. There on the door were two pieces of paper. One paper had the names of the kids who would go on to play the team. The other dreaded list had the names of the kids who were going to have to come back and try again next year.

My name was not on either list. I tried out as a defensive lineman all of camp. I always wanted to be on the defensive side of the ball. My favorite player growing up was cornerback and safety Ronnie Lott. He would just punish people with the hardest hits.

I remember one year when Ronnie was injured, and the doctor said he would be out with a hand cast for two weeks. He told them he was playing no matter what. The doc told him almost jokingly that he would have to amputate the finger if he really wanted to play.

Ronnie told him to go ahead and do it then. He did and played that week. I wanted to play football with that mentality. I wanted to play defense like Ronnie Lott. I wanted the stats, the hype, and everything that came with it.

Somewhat confused on the tryout results, I sat with the Nassau head coach, and he explained that they already had too many defensive players. However, he noticed a gift in me and did not want to see my talent disappear. The coach offered me a position on the offensive line. It was not my preference, but if it meant I could play, then so be it.

There were some adjustments I had to make if I was going to be successful at this new position. I would start playing the offensive line and approaching it with a defensive mentality—doing it my own way.

As a personal motivational tool, I started to keep track of the stats that the team does not, tallying up in my head every time I flattened someone on their back, kept a successful block, or broke an opponent's spirit. I also wanted to enjoy every moment of the experience. I never thought about going pro back then; I just wanted to play one game at a time.

This would go on to be a special transition in my life. Nassau was one of the best junior college teams in the tristate area. We were a strong and diverse team. The roster was built with players mostly from the East Coast.

A lot of my teammates originated from dangerous and rough communities, neighborhoods that gave few options to its kids. You either hustled on the streets or played sports. Those pressures create a unique character in someone. A very hardened, proud, and fearless fighter is forged under those pressures.

That's who we were battling against at practice every day. We were not just competing for the chance to play on game day; we were pushing to advance socially. We fought to have something better than what we were surrounded by in those neighborhoods back home.

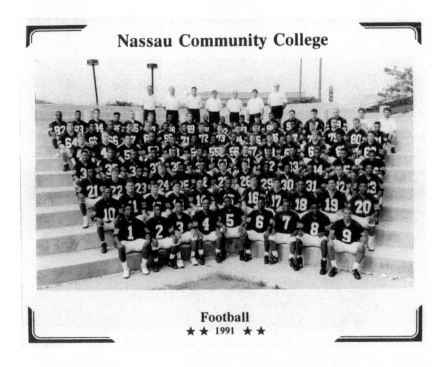

Nassau Community College

Football
★ ★ 1991 ★ ★

The Nassau football program has a reputation for extremely competitive play and coaching. This was at the core of our team and the generations before us. I was now ready to contribute to that legacy, and it would prove to be a challenge from the get-go.

I'll never forget my first practice during my freshman year at Nassau. I was watching all the players carefully and taking mental notes about each one of them. Everyone looked like real men, not college students.

I couldn't take my eyes off this beast of a player. He was a fifth-year vet in a two-year school and commanded every aspect of the football team. He was jacked! Everything that you thought about when picturing a professional player was embodied in this young "vitamin"-filled specimen.

The sun was cooking the field as we cycled through our regimented drills. I was up next in a full-contact drill. This particular drill is where a player had to force the other player past the line of scrimmage. If you could impose your will on the player and dominate them, then you win the drill. Easier said than done, of course.

I was shaking in my boots when I dropped down into my stance. As fate would have it, waiting at the other end of the drill was the player I described earlier. This was not a person; it was a monster wearing a helmet and pads, waiting to run right through me. Although he was already in my head, I knew I had to stay focused. How I handled this situation would define me moving forward.

What a way to start your day. We were lined up, got down, and ready to fire. We both had our mean faces poised, and our eyes locked on each other. Ready, set, go.

The truth is, I was so damn scared that when the coach blew the whistle, I uncoiled out of my stance like a rocket. I hit him so hard and fast that he pancaked on his back. Everyone went crazy as the laughs roared from the circle of doom. With my head down, I trotted to the end of the drill line, thinking, *Thank God that's over.*

However, it wasn't. My new friend popped up off the ground, stunned and foaming at the mouth, yelling, "Get that rookie back here now. Nobody does that to me." Soon my coach's voice found and commanded me, "*Brown!* Get back to the front of the line!"

Without hesitation, I traced my steps back to the front. Not only did I poke the bear, but I really pissed him off. I had a history of being singled out, as you read earlier. My high school experience prepared me to face the fear head-on.

It was guaranteed he was going to be coming at me even harder after I embarrassed him. This time, I dropped back into my stance and looked at the coach through the corner of my eye, trying to time the whistle perfectly to give myself as much of an advantage as I could.

Digging my cleat into the soft, quiet earth, I waited as a patient tiger would, ready to pounce. I yearned to hear the coach's coffee breath create the unmistakable siren that blared from the shiny steel whistle. *Go!* I hit him with everything I had and flattened him out again.

I learned right then and there that if you're bigger and stronger than me, I am going to be faster than you, and if you're faster than me, I'm going to put myself in a position to be stronger than you. If you are stronger and faster than I am, I'm going to be smarter than you.

This was the key to my success on the field, and it started with that victory at practice. To think I almost didn't make the team. It's so important that kids know that there are going to be moments in life that you trip or even completely fall along the journey. It's crucial to stick to what you believe in and push forward to better yourself.

We need to empower our youth to at least try even when the odds are against them. It will help make them graceful champions and, even more importantly, accept the agony of defeat.

Chapter 4

DRAFTED

The January frost still covered all the windows as I buckled in with a chill. I settled my large frame into the back seat of my parents' car, sitting quietly as the tires rhythmically met the grooves in the highway while leaving Long Island.

I think we were trying to be strong for our own reasons on the car ride to Georgia Tech. We all knew that today was my first time moving out of the house and heading off to college. I was transferring from Nassau Community College to Georgia Tech, and it still had not fully set in.

I would have been a great Division 2 or 3 player after my success at Nassau. I never had thought about Division 1 as a possibility, and that was the big time.

My high school coach wanted me to go to Southern CT (Division 2), whose football team had a losing record of 1 and 10 or 2 and 9. There wasn't anything exciting about that for me since my high school team was also coming off losing records the past couple of seasons. As a kid, you dream of bigger stages to perform on.

Regardless, I was intimidated to go to any college. Graduating high school kicked my butt enough. I wasn't thinking about more school. My mother always said, "If we can afford it, we will send you." She stood by the fact that all her kids needed to at least get an associate's degree.

Needless to say, I still expected to see mom cry that day. It's what mamas do, especially my beautiful mother. Bettie was from a dirt-road community in Emporia, Virginia. She wielded her old-school soul like a mighty sword. It was there to protect the most important thing to her throughout her whole life: her family.

She was the youngest of twelve growing up. And on that day, she was watching her firstborn son go away to college. I know she was proud that I was continuing to respect her wishes of educational pursuit.

I sure as heck wasn't going to cry, though. I was going to be playing Division 1 football. I was on my way to becoming an elite athletic specimen and an independent one. I carried a very strong presence with me everywhere I went. That was the New Yorker in me. Not saying we are better or worse, but we are just a little different.

I was so excited that first day I arrived at my new campus. Bring on the party! The first thing I was going to do was get a tattoo and an earring! My father said I was never to get one under his roof, and today was the day that all changed. It's funny what you focus on as young adults.

We finally arrived and transferred all my life's essentials from the family car to the dorm room. I had such an electricity about me. I was so excited to be here. Eventually, my parents left and headed back to Long Island.

The creaking steel door closed me into my empty, cold room. It also felt like it closed me into my new reality. I was surrounded by boxes of who I once was. Unpacking them would be the start of who I would become next.

Now I was alone both physically and emotionally. I was actually scared. I had arrived ahead of the start of the next semester and was one of the few students on the vast campus. The existing football team was finishing up in Hawaii at the national championship, and I was counting down the minutes until we were united. Being on a team is also a security blanket when you need support.

I was also alone inside. All the freedom in the world couldn't fill that place in my heart for my family. I'm the oldest of four, and I always felt that I had to set an example and be there for my siblings.

Today I just sat and cried my eyes out. I could not help it; my emotions were so strong. My emotions were just as strong when I played football, and I would lean on that during my transition.

I wasn't thinking about the NFL. I was only thinking about being great in the next practice or the next game. I was really good at playing "in the moment" when I was younger. I focused on handling one problem at a time, one player at time, and one day at a time.

Now I was here and did not even know how to work the phone to order a pizza. I didn't even know if they had pizza here. I was panicking. The irony was my parents were fine. We laughed about it during my first visit home.

It was also the first time my mother saw the famous tattoo and earring I acquired. She would put me in my place, saying, "I sent you away to college to get smarter, and here you came back, dumber than when you left." Ha!

I learned a lot in those two years at Georgia Tech. I was able to experience some of the aspects of luxury in a Division 1 university. The training facilities were an important part of the experience. When I entered the sprawling iron paradise, it was like something you would see on TV.

Every detail was meticulously thought of. The space sprawled for what seemed like miles. There was wall-to-wall matting and mirrors, creating the perfect border for these superior tools of strength. There were Georgia Tech logos on every disk and dumbbell, reminding you of the greatness that was expected of you. All the iron was racked abundantly, mathematically, and with care. You felt stronger just standing there.

GARY BROWN
Brentwood, N.Y.

Where I come from, the gyms were small storage rooms. We were not one of the larger universities who had the facilities and budgets to provide high-quality accommodations for their students. We came from the raw and gritty gyms in Nassau Community College. It was almost like a medieval training camp.

The grit of those earlier gyms mirrored the grit of the players using them. Whether at Nassau or Georgia Tech, there was always a line of players behind you, waiting for you to make a mistake. There was always someone trying to take your job, and they were hungry to play. These young men already looked like they were playing in the NFL. They just needed a shot to be seen.

I had a very successful two-year career playing football there. It flew by so quickly. Georgia Tech was a special place to me. There was a chance I would be moving elsewhere depending on how the draft went, but I wasn't giving it much thought.

I was projected to be a possible walk-on somewhere at best. That would mean trying out for a team if nobody chose me in the main NFL draft. You have to really be motivated to try out for any team when knowing that they already made their top picks for the upcoming season.

The competition was thick to enter pro football, and there were five other teammates of mine that were supposed to be drafted before me. There are so few players chosen out of the thousands across the country playing college football. I came to terms with my fate regardless of the situation.

Before the draft, an unexpected breakup with my girlfriend had a major impact on me. I was crushed. Determined to move on, I found peace and an escape in lifting weights. I focused day in and day out on my training, and it started to show.

While the scouts were at the school, looking at their predetermined players on their clipboards, they couldn't help but notice me out there. If they were competing in a speed drill, I was next to them, doing the same one. If they were showcasing their strength in the gym, I was a couple stations down, giving everything I had. I felt I had nothing to lose.

I started getting some attention. I didn't think much of it because I was not doing it to get noticed; I was doing it to heal my heart. However, it would become an important detail in my journey to the draft.

In 1994, during the draft, there was a little scrolling ticker at the bottom of the screen on ESPN. If you were selected by an NFL team, you had to sit and wait for your name to come across the rolling list. If you missed it, you were out of luck and had to wait to catch it again in fifteen minutes.

None of the top five guys on my Georgia Tech team were drafted yet, and the draft was winding down. This came as a surprise to them and also meant I definitely didn't have a chance to be selected.

Already coming to terms with this, I wasn't going to stick around just to be disappointed. I went about my business, enjoying the last moments with my college friends. We went out on the town.

The next morning, I was getting calls to my dorm room saying I was going to be drafted. I didn't believe it for a second. My teammates used to do that to each other all the time at Georgia Tech. Leaving falsely recorded messages of congratulations for getting into the NFL was a pretty common prank. This morning was no different, and I wasn't going to give in now. With a throbbing headache from the night before, I fell back asleep.

That all changed when my agent called. He yelled at me, explaining that there were NFL coaches trying to get a hold of me. I couldn't believe it. I was officially being drafted by the Pittsburgh Steelers.

The Packers were next on the clock and said they were going to take me if the Steelers did not. I thought, *Look, Mama, I made it!* I couldn't celebrate until I saw my name come across that slow rolling list on ESPN. I was drafted in the fifth round, pick 148 to Pittsburgh Steelers. After it was official, I packed up my dorm room and headed home, staying there until training camp started.

The Pittsburgh Steelers football team and community clicked with me right away. I loved it there. I worked my butt off every day at practice, trying to earn my spot on the team.

I found myself battling with defensive legends Kevin Greene and Greg Lloyd along with their highly motivated linemen. There was such a difference in the games' intensity and physical competition at the NFL level both on and off the field. These players are the best in the world.

I appreciated learning the small nuances of the big-market team, especially when they directly impacted me. During training camp, the defensive captains would pick a rookie on the defensive side and take them out for dinner and drinks. This was to welcome them in and to get to know them a little better before the season started. They chose differently for some reason this year.

I was in my dorm after practice when I got the knock. It was Kevin Greene and Greg Lloyd standing outside my door.

"Come on, Gary. We are taking you out for dinner," they yelled.

I sat cautiously on my bed, replying, "Nope, not falling for it. Thanks, but no thanks."

This went on for about fifteen minutes as I stood firm, denying them any chance to haze me as a rookie offensive lineman.

Finally, Coach Bill Cowher came to the door, and that got me to open up. He told me it was okay and to go with them. He assured me that their intentions were good. What an incredible opportunity to have come true considering how it could have gone if they were there to give me a hard time.

They respected my work ethic on the field and stamina behind a shot glass. We threw drinks back all night long, chopping it up. I knew they had a good time hanging out with me, but somewhere in the back of their minds, they were going to wear me out for the next day's battle at the line of scrimmage.

They were wrong about that. I made sure I was on the field before anyone in order to welcome them to practice. I'll never forget that night. The peer mentorship and acceptance was huge. It brings a team closer together when the members feel part of the football family. You are willing to work harder for the captains and for yourself.

My time in Pittsburgh was short, and Green Bay picked me up off waivers before I could sign a practice squad contract with the Steelers. And just like that, I was headed to a place I didn't even know where to point out on a map. I was scared again.

If you're from Long Island, there is not much that can get you to travel the country, let alone leave the area. I'm from New York and thought I would stay there forever or at least close by. Georgia was a stretch when I made the move to college.

As my plane touched down in this strange, new place, I noticed that I stood out. If there was another person with dark skin, they were likely headed to the same place I was—Lambeau Field.

I arrived at my room, and the first thing I did was call my mother and tell her where my hotel was in case it was the last place I was seen. I told her the name of the news station across the street, my room number, and to pray for me.

This feeling would soon go away, but upon first experiencing it, I realized this was a big step for me. It would also begin a long road of sacrifice and hard work to keep my football dream alive.

Once settled into the town, I understood what they meant when they said Green Bay is one of the NFL's best-kept secrets. The people there love football and love the people who play it. It is the heartbeat of the community. They live from Sunday to Sunday. There is so much support and pride that comes from everyone there. It was incredible.

After all that happened in Pittsburgh, I was now on the field in Green Bay. Even at the NFL level, there is a high man and low man on the totem pole. I was once again starting my climb up from the bottom.

The competition you face makes you better. You always want to cut your teeth against the best in order to be the best. I was trading Hall of Famers in Pittsburgh for one of the all-time greats here in Green Bay: Reggie White.

If you don't know who that is, you will not have to look far. He was one of the most incredible men I have ever met. He was a sweet and spiritual man with a kind heart. He worked his butt off every minute, and it showed. Regardless of how nice he was off the field, when it came to football business, he was laser-focused. Reggie was a beast on the field and the absolute highest man on the pole.

It was the first week of football, and I was already starting to make an impression with my new teammates. First, it was a player who had a lot in common with me. We were both fierce competitors and destined for a confrontation from the start. We had the same initials, drove the same white truck, and even had the same "G. Brown" on the license plate.

This is a tough guy's sport, and we were both tough as nails. Eventually, those practices and seasons together make you stronger as teammates through that unique bond.

This team was rich in culture, and the more time you are there the more you know. There was an unwritten rule as the season started that drill work at practice moved at 50 to 75 percent for the veterans. This prepared them for game day, where they would unleash 110 percent of whoop ass on their opponents.

I was about as new as could be and had not yet learned the nuances of the training camp. My coach sent me out to the huddle with a head full of steam. They told me I was working for a job and had to earn it. They said I better not go at half speed, or I would be on the next plane home.

I lined up against him, and when the ball was hiked, I fired off and hit him with everything I had. Surprised and pissed, he had a lot of specific words for the coaches on why the hell I was going full speed. Deviously, the coaches gave me the same order and a reminder about losing my spot if I did not go at full speed.

The second play went similarly to the first, and when the ball hiked, I fired at him again. This time, we got into a physical tussle after the play. I was starting to read the writing on the wall, and it did not translate well for me.

In the third play, I was lined up against the late and great Reggie White. They called for a backside-toss running play. All I had to do was step in front of him and keep him from getting to the other side of the backfield, where the quarterback was. This should be an easy play for me as I studied him all the time. I tried to understand how and when he would move.

I was trying to keep my job, so I came at him aggressively. He did not appreciate this any more than my other buddy did, and he let me know it. He was like a lion issuing a stern warning, growling at me with his unforgettably deep and raspy voice.

The fourth play was a pass play, and I was still lined up against Reggie. He was a defensive mastermind and was specifically famous for his specialty "club" move that he did. Hearing the quarterback yell "*Hike!*" was like lighting the fuse of an explosive. The play went off, and so did he.

He hit me with his massive arm, getting his hands under my pads and lifting my feet off the ground. In a game, he would have proceeded to slam the opponent onto the ground and feast on the ball carrier. Without letting his grip or control of me go, he now had my undivided attention. Now he was close enough to read my mind and asked me if I was going to step it back during the drills. I politely said, "Yes, Mr. White," and trotted back to the huddle.

The laughs came as soon as my feet left the ground and didn't stop even as I prepared for the next play. It was at that moment I earned their respect, and it was probably why I made the team. Time seemed to fly after that.

As a kid growing up watching the sport on TV, I was blessed to actually walk onto that same field with the best athletes in the world. I felt accomplished in my career, playing for Nassau and eventually Georgia Tech. To get into the NFL was a dream come true.

I think it's important for kids to know that no matter what level you are playing at, you need to be in the moment. Appreciate the teammates around you and appreciate the opportunity that you have. The victories are just as special at the Pop Warner level as they are in the NFL.

Football is about making you a better player as well as a better person. Be the best you can be, and the best situation will present itself to you both on and off the field.

Chapter 5

CROWD NOISE

Playing sports when growing up in the '70s and '80s was so interesting because of the diversity we grew up around. It's like we were in the middle of a war. Our neighborhood was the melting pot. Across the main road were the predominantly White communities. On the other side was Regis Park, a predominantly Black neighborhood. Both had drugs and violence; they were just hidden behind different colors.

We were in the middle and had Palestinian, Arabian, Chinese, Indian, and Haitian people and everyone else. The diversity was important for us to experience as kids. All we really wanted to do anyway was play. We played hockey, soccer, and lacrosse against the White kids. We played handball and baseball against the Spanish kids and football and basketball against the Black neighborhoods.

We stuck together as a unit from hood to hood. If you knocked one of us out, we'd knock one of you out. We all know where we came from and still stick together to this day. We are a special band of brothers. Our crew put Garnet Park on the map, and we represented it like we owned it.

As life went on, I would learn that the country was as divided as those small neighborhoods on Long Island. It's a division that would put me in some scary situations as a Black man. These situations of inequality became very noticeable to me within the school sports system as well.

I graduated in '89. In '85–'86, my school went from predominantly White to predominantly Black. Then it became predominantly Puerto Rican. At one point, we had the third highest population in the world of Puerto Rican people, first being Puerto Rico, second being Florida, and then our little town, Brentwood.

Our head coaches in school were all mostly White. This was the cause of some underlying tensions between them and the players. Other White players were getting blatantly favored. I remember this one kid who played my position. He was a senior while I was a junior, and I was way better than him.

The coaches had me in the trenches doing all the grunt work and moving the team down the field on offense. As soon as we were in scoring position, the coach would put in the less talented senior to give him exposure. It made it hard for guys like me to get my talent noticed if I was taken out during the big plays. Back then, we were rarely filmed, but when we were, it was to promote us to colleges in order to play at the next level.

This happened all the time. The same treatment was given to me during other sports like basketball and baseball. Mean-spirited coaches have too much power. If they don't like the way you walk or talk, then they can hold it against you without any repercussions.

You rely on your instincts when you are placed in these situations, situations where you are doing nothing wrong and yet you are accused or attacked while you're helpless. People of color are bullied and, worse yet, guilty until proven innocent. For some reason, we just keep on taking it and hoping it could be the last time that it happens. Unfortunately, we know it's almost impossible that it will be the last time. If racism has lasted this long, what could possibly end it now?

Twenty years later, it was not my coaches I was worried about anymore. I was now worried about unethical authorities abusing their power. I can recall several instances that I feared for my personal safety despite my size and strength.

One night, I took my girl out to dinner for her birthday. I let her enjoy a couple of drinks, and I was the driver. I had a glass of wine with dinner because the food was so good. We were having such a fun and romantic night; it was the perfect birthday party for her.

It was early on in my rehab from my back surgery, and I was physically suffering. At this point, it was very difficult to get around. I hobbled awkwardly on a thin wooden cane to leave the restaurant that night.

We got into the Expedition and headed for home. We were still riding a natural high from her birthday dinner. I had traveled so much during my career, so it was awesome to finally have some time together. As we began our journey home, a cop car flew past us, going the opposite direction. They were speeding back toward the restaurant.

Suddenly our fantasy was going to turn into a nightmare. In an instant, the mood was over. Alternating red and blue lights started playing a devastating drum roll in my rearview mirror. Nobody likes to get pulled over. Whenever you are in that position, those feelings of fear flood your gut. I knew I was not doing anything wrong, and yet here I was, pulled over. I was a Black man in a big fancy car. I could have been a doctor for all they knew.

Turned out, they did know me. Within a couple of seconds, we were stopped, and I heard the first cop saying my name as he crept closer and closer to the door.

"Gary Brown."

What were the chances he was a fan?

As the cold air from the crisp winter night slowly poured into the exposed car, I was still leaking a nervous sweat. They were asking me a ton of questions that didn't make sense. Next, they wanted me to get out and take a field sobriety test. I could barely get in and out of the truck as it was, let alone do a damn test.

I kept on asking him to just take me into the station because I was not physically able to complete the test. Finally, they agreed. No matter what, I knew I was being arrested. I just wanted to get it over with.

Before we left, they pulled my car into a dark, empty lot. The window was still down, and my girl was freezing. The cop extended his hand, briefly offering the keys to her so she could turn on the heat and stay warm. Once the bait was set, he pulled his hand back mockingly.

"What do you think I am, an idiot? You're not getting these."

They took me. They left her. Can you believe that? She had to walk all the way back to the restaurant alone to try and get a ride home, all while I was being taken to the station unnecessarily for further harassment.

It is a helpless feeling. It's really confusing being so physically strong and in situations like that where you are completely powerless. Even my celebrity status did not get me equal treatment. I wish that these incidents were few and far between, but that was not the case. After all was said and done that night, I was released with no charges.

One year in Green Bay, Wisconsin, I was in town early for training. Some of the other players and I hit the local shooting range after practice. I had a legal and fully registered pistol I used to use for sport shooting.

After the range, we all wanted to go out. I left my Cherokee parked for the night, not wanting to drink and drive. There was no trunk in the SUV, and lawmakers did not have any rules yet about firearm placement in the vehicle.

We went out for a night that did not last as long as we first thought. I got dropped back off at my car and headed to another friend's house. We didn't have GPS back then, so I was using written directions with a map from the glove box.

A cop saw me pulling over onto the shoulder and spun around behind me. He pulled me over because he said I was swerving. I explained to him what I was looking for and that I was about five houses from my destination. He did not care.

He asked to search my car. I asked him why and for what. I also kept asking why I was being pulled over since I was not swerving. Now they wanted me to get out of the car. I kept pleading with them, quietly asking why. Finally, I said, "To hell with it," and let them search the car. I remembered the gun and verbally told them it was in the back of the SUV. Despite my transparency, all hell broke loose.

They took my completely legal and registered gun away. They had me out of the car now with batons drawn. They were threatening me that, despite my towering physical presence, they could still take me out. I continued to plead that it was not necessary to do that and that I would continue to cooperate.

"You are being arrested," they spat viciously.

Nobody wants to be in this situation and under this emotional stress. On top of it, they cared not about causing physical pain to my body. They had my bulky, muscle-laced arms wrenched as far behind my back as they could go.

The metal was digging into my thick wrists, creating a searing pain. Next, they threw me in the back of the cop car facedown. I was now helpless and starting to panic. They manipulated my legs into a ninety-degree angle, twisted my foot, and wedged it into the doorframe. *Slam.*

I was now packed into the back of the car with no breathing room. I am extremely claustrophobic, and it was escalating with the physical discomfort and shortness of air. I was a ticking time bomb and wished it were over.

After I was released, I went straight to the stadium. I spoke with my coaches and some of the team's staff. I told them what happened and asked them what they were going to do about it. I was deflated as they chose to do nothing. It fell on deaf ears. They said they would see what they could do to resolve it but strongly suggested that I just move on.

Even as of this day, there is no record of the arrest, and they took my gun. I was told if I wanted to keep my job, I would forget that it happened. Easy for them to say. They weren't wrongly pulled over and forced into a tin can facedown.

This is a people problem. We need to do better for each other, specifically the unarmed people of color being killed by armed authorities. It's a vicious cycle of unwarranted violence against inno- cent people because of the way they look.

The situation is so complicated. It is so important that we raise awareness on these issues so that we can flush the evils out of these systems. We as a people need to be able to have dialogues with one another and really listen. I know I am not perfect, but who is? One thing's for sure: I don't deserve to be profiled and set at a constant disadvantage, a societal disadvantage that could cost me my life because of how I look. Nobody deserves that.

I always use the Serenity Prayer to get me through the toughest days, the days where you are being attacked and you decide to battle through it with help from God. These confrontations are constantly building that inner champion within us one fight at a time, one moment at a time, and one victory at a time.

This same social hate is present in the sports world as well. You never see it from your couches at home, but there are some ugly aspects to our interactions with certain hate-filled fans. They think a sports ticket gives them a ticket to verbally abuse us. Even though they think they are trying to throw us off our game, they are actually disrespecting us as people.

I can still hear them screaming at us. We were knee-deep in an intense game. The field was more like a fight zone in a gladiator's arena. It was a place where, at times, the fans are more vicious than the players. It's ironic because we were the ones hitting each other at full speed.

In the end, the dollars that roll through the door is what is paramount. The money is what matters most to the owners. We are there to take whatever abuse they give us in all aspects of the sport whether we like it or not.

That included the rough racial slurs that were being hurled at me and my fellow Black teammates. It was a superfan couple who had the best seats in the house: right behind our bench. They were so close that if I had a french fry, I could have dipped it in their ketchup-filled white cardboard boat.

That couple had a playbook with one play in it. The plan that day was to mentally derail us while morally derailing themselves. Every racial slur in the book was being maliciously fired at us, and if you looked at the scoreboard, it might have seemed to be working.

Before we came out of the locker room from halftime, there was a hope that maybe they went home during the break. What were the chances they would only stay for the first half? Just as the sun rises and sets, there they were. It was as if they themselves rested during halftime because they were back at it in full strength.

We had a job to do. Our team needed to win on the field, and we as people needed to win in the arena of perseverance. When you are being beat down emotionally and socially, you need to lower your shoulders and get to work. That had to happen in this game as well. Play after play, we tightened up and pushed forward. Nothing was being given to us. Everything had to be earned.

We were fighting back as if our lives depended on it. Unfortunately, our lives do depend on it off the field. If these people were acting like this during a public football game, what do you think they were doing at home and with their friends?

Back in the game, we were giving up no ground, inching the score closer and closer. We tied the game 20–20 in a final push. It sent the competition into overtime, which meant our superfans were going to get more time to demean us.

The two teams battled on. There was time for one more series, and we were down by a score. We marched down the field and capitalized on a game-winning drive in overtime—a field goal that sailed through the bright yellow uprights. We won 23–20.

Stunned. Silent. Success. We did what nobody thought was possible. We took a beating in the first half and clawed our way back to victory.

We took the napalm blast of racism from that sad couple. We absorbed their poisonous conversation and did not negatively react to it. Instead, we kicked their team's ass and walked off winners in every aspect. By silencing their team, we silenced them and all the evil they stood for.

These people are an example of how backward things are. They used so much energy filled with hate to try and get in our heads. They loved their team so much that they used words that hurt so much to hear in a public setting, a family setting, hell, any setting. It is embarrassing and sad. I wonder if anyone else around felt as sorry for them as I did.

Whether we won or lost that game, we left there having to take the higher ground in that situation. The sad part is those people had to leave there with each other, missing out on a powerful aspect of life, and that is called true unity—the opportunity to safely and spiritually live with one another. Until they realize that for them-selves, they will have to carry that heavy weight of hatred for the rest of time.

The victory was sweeter that day because we earned it not just for ourselves but for every other person of color out there who has had to fight through an experience like that and lost—a person who did not make it home to their families after a fatal night, people who are held back from opportunity and a quality of life because of the way they look, people who are held back from feeling equal, and people who are deprived of feeling like we all belong here together, like we all matter.

It is important to also understand the power of sports in this situation. It is a common ground that can help defeat that racist stigma. I had a teammate in college who came from a small country town where there were no Black people. The only people of color he saw were on TV.

We got along so well on the team, and yet if I came back to his hometown, there would be a lot of questions asked of him. I wonder if he would tell them all that we were both just two men that were friends because of what we accomplished on the field. Would he say that we were two men who were friends? Words and actions matter to everyone.

We are all different, and we need to embrace that. We need to talk to one another more often. We need to listen to one another. If we can start to do that, then we can make it together.

> In tough situations, the serenity prayer is everything to me. (Gary Brown)

> The Serenity Prayer
> God, grant me the serenity to accept the things I cannot change, the courage to change the things I can, and the wisdom to know the difference. Amen.

Chapter 6

SPANKED BY THE COMMUNITY

Times were different then. People were more aware of being accountable for themselves. For me, that mindset was developed when we were kids. If you messed up, Aunt Rose was sending you to her room to get her belt. Imagine that: getting sent to choose the weapon you were going to get hit with.

I recall gripping the cold metal sliding door and slowly pushing it over, revealing the makeshift armory. I remember standing in her closet, holding a thick leather three-hole belt with a large buckle on it. I did not see this choice going too well, so I moved it aside and settled on a small skinny belt. Man, was I wrong; that thing could have cut through steel and made me think twice about all my choices from then on.

In addition to our tight family unit, we were also raised by our community. I guess I should say we were beaten by the whole community. If you misbehaved at one of the other houses on the block, you would get disciplined by that family. After they beat you, they would bring you home and tell your family what you did wrong, and then you would get beat by your actual parents.

I remember Miss Jackson shoving me down the block to my front yard, yelling, "Betty, I had to beat your son. He was cussing!"

Out came my mother to give me a second beating because she was mad that Miss Jackson had to beat me. It's funnier now than it was then.

38

I can remember the moments leading up to the last time I got spanked. My father was at PJ's barbershop, getting cleaned up, when they saw a group of drug dealers forming outside. This was the late '70s, and it was a common occurrence in Amityville. These men were hustling, and he knew they should not have been. It was up to the elders and the old-school guys to handle these situations on the street.

PJ told them over and over again, "You can do that shit at home, at the other end of the street, or at the other end of the block but not in front of my shop."

Time and time again, they did not listen. One day, the old guys had enough, and out of the shop they came.

Silently and with purpose, my father and PJ moved like music toward the door. On his way out, he turned and looked at us with a stern warning: "Sit down and don't move!" They drew the shades shut and delivered their message. We popped the shades open and watched my father and his friend beat the hell out of all those guys. That was all I needed to see.

I respected my father because he was cool and he was correct. He took care of his family and his community and set a positive example for us growing up. His nickname was T-Bone. I remember his smile as he jingled, "You can call me Tommy, you can call me Brown, but don't call me T-Bone when I ain't around!"

Sometime after the barbershop incident, I remember getting spanked for something stupid. My father came out of the room, holding his wrist and grimacing. My mother asked him what was wrong, clearly seeing he had hurt his hand from the spanking.

"I hurt my hand. I need to start hitting that boy like a man," he growled.

I knew what that meant because I witnessed it firsthand at the barbershop when he hit those other men like men. Needless to say, that was the last time I got a spanking because I didn't want any of that trouble.

I am not condoning physical discipline, but I believe understanding consequences can save kids from bad situations. It can stop you in your tracks and make you think twice about what you are doing.

Sometimes all you need is that split second to change your mind. Our prisons are full of people who should have stopped and thought, probably wishing they could have chosen differently. We need that extra moment to think about consequences as we are imperfect people with a lot going on in our lives, especially kids who are often on stimulation overload.

When you had a problem with someone in school, you made sure it was actually a "problem." Back then, it was guaranteed you were all meeting in the parking lot after class to settle it.

When I was wrong or misspoke, I got punched in my face for it. Kids these days hide behind devices and do not know how powerful or hurtful their words can be when delivered person-to-person.

It is a real problem in our society and among our youth. A huge lack of respect lives in this generation, and it is because parents are not disciplining their kids. Again, I am not promoting violence. I am promoting parents getting their kids to stop and think before they act or speak. We need to help them understand that consequences need to be respected.

We need to prepare our kids to learn how to deal with that pit in your stomach—that unmistakable feeling when you're faced with a tough decision and the anxiety that comes on in a wave. Teach them what that feeling is and let them know it is okay to have it. Most importantly, teach them how to process it in a healthy way. Having the confidence to make positive decisions under pressure can help them through so much in life.

Sports helped prepare me emotionally in so many ways. Playing sports taught me how to handle victories and losses with pride. It taught me how to fall down alone and get back up again. It also helped me understand winning with professionalism and accomplishing goals as a team. When you are a part of something bigger than yourself, you have to be accountable for your actions. That is true about your family, your team, and your community.

I have seen a lot of negative situations while growing up, and they are the driving forces to help me change that for any child I work with. Change is not immediate; it takes time. So we need to lean on each other during that battle. Positive repetition and taking responsibility for ourselves add up in a good way.

Our parents are not always going to be there in those pivotal moments. How they have prepared us to handle them is what will matter most. Nobody really wants to believe they have more to learn. We often think we know it all already.

In the story of our lives, the learning moments are the ones that matter most. Behind every victory is a struggle. How you handle yourself and help others along the way is what will define you. I saw these situations all the time during my football career.

In football, a short-term memory is both a good and bad thing. Obviously, with enough mistakes, you're going to get released from the team. However, if you have the resilience necessary to learn from the previous play, the previous game, and the previous season, then you will be well equipped to continue your career while striving for victory. It is almost impossible to achieve perfection, but keep in mind it's perfectly okay to strive for consistent excellence.

We need to talk to each other more as people as well. It will help us learn from our mistakes and experiences. I was in a tough-guy business. We never talked to the media about our personal lives. Shoot, they knew enough. What they knew usually involved only the bad stuff you didn't want them to know. In the locker room, it was different.

We shared more with each other. It helped make us stronger and kept us mentally healthy. There is nothing I miss more about the game than that team bond, a unique atmosphere that oftentimes was more like family. We took that unity with us onto the field through thick and thin.

Even though you are on a team, you still have to be account-able for your own actions and decisions. The pressure sometimes is greater because it impacts more than just yourself. You are constantly accountable whether you are away from the stadium or during prac-tice and especially on game days. For me, one game stands out in particular.

It was deafening in the stadium. We were playing at Minnesota in week 4 of our Super Bowl season. Vikings fans are already so intense, but that year, their team was undefeated. The roars sounded like they filled the stadium with actual Vikings. It was going to be a bloodbath, a battle won only by those willing to sacrifice it all.

As we took the field, we were ready to write history. We were preparing to add to the rivalries' existing epic clashes as we trotted onto the battlefield. There was no love lost between us. It would go on to be one of the most physical games I have ever played in.

We were up 21–17 in the fourth quarter, but the game was far from over. And I would be handed an unexpected life lesson that I will never forget.

The Vikings' defensive coordinator came at me all of first quarter, all of second quarter, and all of third quarter and always with someone new. They were sending the beefy guys, the real bull rushers. They came at me the entire game, always putting fresh legs on me, trying to wear me down.

If you hit me, then I would hit you right back. Play after play, I was just earning my keep on every down. When I first entered the NFL, I was very motivated, curious, and strong. Now I was a starting lineman for my team, and my strength came from that daily fight to keep my job. I'm a kid from Long Island, so everything that I did, I did it to put us on the map for all the right reasons.

Don't get me wrong. Sometimes things just happen. Mike or Brett had the call set perfectly on that particular play. We had the game set up for the win.

I had my eyes locked on the tackle, which, at the time, was John Randle. John was one of, if not the most, dominant players I've ever faced. He would go on to become a Hall of Famer. On that day, we squared up on the frozen soil with the game on the line. On that day, he was my problem.

I turned away, trying to look him off. The running back was going to come out of the backfield with one job, and that was to chip-block Randall. We all knew Randall was an animal, so he was going to be coming after him hard. On paper, Brett would just drift to the right a little bit as he came in, and all the players would be going to the right. He was going to toss the football right over his head and run it right into the end zone for the win. After that, we were going to run out of the stadium like, "Yes, we did it!" Like I said, on paper, that was the plan.

Hike! The running back went the wrong way, so John Randle was free to run. I just left him alone because someone else was supposed to be blocking him. That play met *fubar* in a head-on collision.

When the running back goes the wrong way it does three different things:

1. It gives the linebacker the wrong read because the linebacker is going to the right, and the running back is supposed to go to the left.
2. John Randle was coming in with a full head of steam, so the running back was supposed to chip him, disrupting him just enough to buy some time, just enough to get him to break stride and slow down. This way, the quarterback can go through his fakes, turn around, and dump the ball off.
3. The quarterback is supposed to be throwing the ball to the running back, and he totally went the wrong way. So it is a botched play a hundred times over. If he just missed the block, Brett was good enough that he could get the throw off, but he had no one to throw it too.

Big ole John Randle hit Brett with such force. On that play, he stripped the ball and sealed the Vikings' victory.

As we were walking off the field, my coaches said they were going to blame me for that game. With my body aching and head throbbing, I just nodded and headed into the locker room. My teammates knew that we all played hard. The offense knew what the play was and how it got botched, but someone had to be at the bottom of that pile.

The reporters did not even ask what happened. They just started off with me being the reason we lost. I could have explained to them what I just explained to you all, but for what? I took responsibility for it and let them attack me. No one went under the bus but me.

I told them I made the mistake and needed to play better. In this business, it's important to know that if you have the opportunity to continue to play, then you should focus on the next game. The ink was dry on those papers, and I was looking ahead to the next one, but not before the battle with the press was over.

Something else happened regarding the way I handled it. Even though that was hard for me to do, I actually ended up getting so much fan mail from Green Bay. They were telling me to keep my head up and that they were not mad at me for the loss. They were certain I would get back on my feet and keep rocking.

That says a lot about a community and a fan base. They were so invested in the football team and really made me feel like I was part of the family. It really made the difference in my energy going out the next week, and I fought to make them and myself proud.

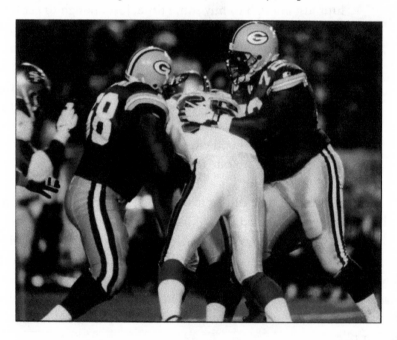

The following week was exhausting. We were feeling the effects of that loss and the physicality of the Vikings game. I was still feeling the fatigue of a double spanking like I was back in the old neighborhood. First, the Vikings beat me, then the media beat me. I got spanked by them both, and I learned how I needed to keep going on. I learned how to overcome tough moments within myself.

I showed the respect my parents taught me. I have the type of personality where I want everyone to like me at least a little bit, and that's what made this a tough lesson. I could have easily mouthed off about the other guys to shift the blame from me to them, but that's not how I was raised. We were built stronger than that.

That positivity is contagious and important because if I had not absorbed that blow from the media, we may not have won the next game. We stayed tight as a group through those challenges and would go on to win the Super Bowl that year. The bigger picture is called the bigger picture because it does not always show the little moments but instead focuses on the end results. We just need to own it and move forward. After all, we only live once, so don't sweat the small stuff. Be proud of your decisions and stay true to yourself.

Chapter 7

SUPER BOWL SUNDAY

Everyone always asks what it was like surrounding the Super Bowl experience. The truth is that we were so exhausted from the grind leading up to that moment that, at times, it almost felt like just another game.

The epic Sunday battles and vigilant practices were coming one after the other, day in and day out. There was also an emotional strain from the endless travel as well. We were constantly moving from one city to another to play.

At times, the travel was a lot for me. I used to get very claustrophobic and still do. I do not like being in small spaces or flying on small planes. I especially do not like small planes.

It was nice with the team, though, because they were not going to squeeze all of us big boys into a puddle jumper. I'll bet the plane rides back then were very different from the ones they have today. Back then, you could do whatever you wanted to. I remember guys smoking cigars, playing cards, and drinking beers on the rides there and home.

There was also a challenge balancing family life during the season for those of us that had families. I was balancing a social life and focusing on football.

When you are living a fast-paced life like that, it often puts personal, physical, and mental health to the wayside. You just keep on moving forward with passionate blinders on to all warnings that you could be wearing yourself down.

Some of those warnings were coming from our bodies as we not only packed our gear from trip to trip but also transported our injured bodies from city to city. You almost felt like you were being held together just long enough to survive and to suit up for the next game. I loved it, though. All of it fit perfectly on my broad shoulders.

Despite all the grueling moments, we were headed to the Super Bowl. We arrived in New Orleans, and I thought, *This is it.* This was the game you wanted to play your whole life if you were involved in football at any level. Even if you did not play football, you still respected the gravity of the game growing up.

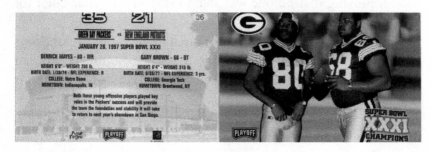

How could you not? Almost every household in America and all over the world fills its living room on that night. Crowds of people cheer on the game, eat party food, and laugh at the commercials. Military bases are filled with soldiers away from their families, and they smile from ear to ear as they watch the games like kids in a candy store.

As a football player, it is the game that stamps you in the history books. It gives you a chance to be part of the greatest team in the world for that year. If you were lucky, you might even do it multiple years in your career. Like anything else, the first one was the hardest to get through, and we were ready for the challenge.

The stage was set. This was where you were going to make those magical catches as the time ran out. This was where you pushed for every inch as you crept closer and closer to the end zone. You mentally prepared yourself so that no matter what defensive player was lined up across from you, you were exploding off the battle line, and you were going to shut them down.

The collective power of two teams and over one hundred players is something to behold. All of our raging spirits were to be engaged for all sixty minutes of battle, sixty minutes that will pass by like sixty seconds. It is like waiting on a roller coaster line for two hours, and the ride lasts but a short moment. It was very important to be present in the moment despite how quickly it passed.

At the end of it all, when the smoke clears, only one team will get to hold up the heralded Lombardi Trophy. The timeless photographs from every previous Super Bowl of the players holding it above their heads in celebration say it all. The trophy is a shiny metal symbol proving that no one was able to stop you in your quest for the world football title.

It is a sign of ultimate respect granted to the victor. It alone pays for all the sacrifices that went into it as a team. No one person can win it alone. You need to be the team who has bonded closer and is healthier than the other team.

Something that is not talked about as much as it should be is the coaching side. Imagine being the coach who has to harness that championship focus within these grown men. All the coaches were tasked with trying to control the nerves and excitement to keep the players in the moment just long enough to win.

Sometimes harder than winning the game is trying to keep the wild ones in the hotel room the night before. Veteran presence on the teams and in the locker rooms is so important during these moments. There is a huge value to having seasoned players who might not be at their peak physically but still have the ability to lead from within. These are the players that remain unfazed by the media and are not easily distracted before the big game.

Our coaches did what they should have done. They reminded us what we're made of. All the years of repetition and grueling practices were meant to prepare us for that big moment. All the listening, learning, and application of skill were to pay off here. We bought into the program, truly believing all of it would add up. The total payoff was our grass-stained cleats digging into the field to play in the world's greatest competition.

Our bodies were worn, and our nerves were tall. You would think that we would be conjuring up crazy trick plays and new schemes, but that was not the case. Surprisingly, our coaches went back to the fundamentals we learned in the Pop Warner league—the basics that you started learning the first day you nervously wiggled your helmet on.

I could still see one of my Pop Warner coaches, Henry Simpkins,[1] yelling at me through my awkwardly fit face mask. I was able to run a little bit and throw a little bit, so he was able to identify me as a threat on the field at a young age. Coach Simpkins showed up on registration day to sign his foster kids up for football in my father's league.

My father had taken the league over to save it from falling out. He eventually talked Coach Simpkins into helping him out until he could enlist other coaches to join the team. It was the best move he could have made on a sports and community level.

This is a very important part of my football story. The league was made up of about forty kids at the time. There was no money in the program. My father, with his thinly enlisted staff, were doing all they could to make sure the kids had somewhere to play.

The heart of this league was the families. They were the ones who made it click. Everyone showed up to all the practices and all the games. There was always food in the parking lots afterward, and the focus was on the kids. Every kid was so happy to just be there. We all wanted to have fun together, and nobody ever complained about what position they were playing. All of us did our jobs, and we did it with a smile. With my father, Tommie Brown, as the commissioner, the league went from dead in the water to fully functional with the help of these dedicated coaches and parents.

"Gary emerged as a leader on our team and really took the program on his back." Coach Simpkins smiled during our interview. He

---

[1] Henry Simpkins was interviewed for the book to discuss details of coaching Gary Brown during Pop Warner Football for Brentwood. All quotes are directly taken from that interview.

continued to shower me with incredible memories from that season. "I can remember our first game."

As he would recall it, our team of forty kids from Brentwood were traveling to Sayville to play the first game of the year. Our opponent, Sayville, was a well-established team with a lot of money behind the program. We pulled up into the parking lot slowly. The kids peered from the bus as if arriving on a new planet, and even as kids, they started to notice specific details.

The first observation was that the Sayville team had new shiny helmets and matching uniforms. He recalls one of his kids crying out, "They look like the Washington Redskins coach!" With a chuckle, he noted, "They were right, and we looked more like the little rascals!"

When someone who has very little observes someone who has so much, something happens. There can be sunken feelings of embarrassment or a feeling of missing out. There were even feelings of resentment. As a kid, you'd almost feel belittled before you even fully know why. That is a strange self-induced fear to deal with.

You even think those people might not even appreciate having it because you want it so badly. That is a lot, to be a child processing that in your head before you have to go play in the game. Our home lives were tough enough, and this was supposed to be fun. The coaches had their hands full with trying to get us focused.

The coaches prompted the kids to exit the bus, and they stepped down onto the foreign territory one pace at a time. Each tired foot was wrapped by a worn cleat. Both legs were snug in ripped, stretchy pants. Almost every jersey was different from the others both in color and in imperfect sizing.

The helmets looked like they had been worn by every kid in the world before they were passed down to us. Still, they were set on the task of protecting us kids to the best of their abilities. You can understand why they harbored some doubt from the first impressions they were witnessing.

The coaches confidently locked everyone mentally into the game. One by one, we took the field for warm-ups. It was like a motionless boat catching a breeze in its sail. *Whoosh,* off we went.

After the sixty minutes passed, we had whooped the Sayville team so badly. At first glance, nobody thought the Brentwood kids would last through the first quarter. It turned out that we were so well practiced and fundamentally sound that we cut through the opponents like a hot knife through butter.

We boarded the same bus that we almost didn't exit, but this time, all were smiling. It was now that we understood why the coaches focused on the basics so much. When we got home, the proud team was greeted by all the smiling families who had prepared a meal for the exhausted gladiators.

Nothing is more important than family, and there was no better crowd to share the victory with. When you put together a plan in life, faith and family are really good ones to have on the top of the list. So as an adult getting off the bus outside the famous football dome in New Orleans, I put one foot in front of the other with a smile.

New Orleans was a volcano about to erupt. The Super Bowl was here, and the city embraced it with a grip that would not loosen. The Packers and the Patriots were set to clash on the grandest sports stage of all time. Both teams geared for a merciless battle.

When people pray in large numbers for the same thing, the feeling is that there's a greater chance to produce the spiritual request. Every player was pacing in their hotel room, taking labored, anxious, deep breaths in and out. Every coach was busy confirming last-minute roster spots, strategies, and game plans.

It was time for us to practice what we prepared. We spent the week focusing on our basics. We were about to take the field for the greatest battle of our careers, and we were doing Pop Warner drills. We were visualizing perfect hand placement, quickening our first steps, and staying low. On the hike, we dropped back six inches, staying firm but loose.

All the details my father and Coach Simpkins told us were so important during the biggest game in the world. I recalled them preaching to us that "if you do these drills and perfect these basics, you will be a better player." To buy into that concept as a child was difficult. On TV, they only showed us the flashy stuff. They never showed the hours of tiring practices. For me, it was always about making our coaches and family proud. It was about our team bond. Now I can say that they were all right. It worked.

Every piece of knowledge gained leading up to the game would be a valuable tool and possible advantage. My father and Coach Simpkins always told us to be smart if we wanted to be a good player.

"Go to class, sit there, and shut up, and if you stay long enough, you just might like it," Simpkins sternly growled as he pointed at me.

The level of expertise that goes into winning the Super Bowl doesn't just happen overnight. Every player that wants to develop a stronger football IQ must have the ability to listen and learn.

Outside the city, the world was watching. Televisions were glowing in rooms across the country, magnetically locking in the faces of fans and interested onlookers. The Packers would go on to beat the Patriots in an epic battle by a score of 35–21. It was an incredible game and absolutely unforgettable.

This victory was meant to be shared, shared with my mentors who taught me that fundamentals and family are the keys to success. This was for my Pop Warner coaches who made us believe that with hard work and a unified team, we could win no matter what we looked like. This was for the parents who waited in the parking lot with food and smiles after every practice and game. This was for my mother and father, who would lift up my chin to the sky during the toughest losses, always telling me it was going to be okay and to keep on going. A spiritual debt was paid to every little kid who suited up and contributed over the years, defining what a real team was.

It is important for parents to let their kids have fun and maintain a positive relationship with the sport whether they win or lose. It is crucial to encourage them to grow in a healthy way with themselves and the sport without negativity from their families and to simply have fun. Nobody can guarantee a championship in life, but we can guarantee a positive experience for our children that will benefit their minds, bodies, and souls.

On January 28, 1997, in a living room on Long Island, Coach Simpkins sat watching the biggest football game on earth. As he watched, he smiled. One of the finest young men who he believed in and mentored actually did it—a young man who he saw become a leader for other children while still a child himself, someone who listened to every word that his coaches said and did the work without a single complaint.

"There he is!" I yelled. "Little Gary Brown
won the Super Bowl!" (Coach Henry Simpkins)

Chapter 8

DAMAGED GOODS

The body is temporary, but the mind is forever. We go through life in hopes of a delicate balance for both. When you are young, you can easily recover from physical injury. The body knows how to heal and fast. During our youth, we have a harder time dealing with our emotions—the extreme waves of disappointment, sadness, and anger.

It's funny how that flips when you are older. Your body does not mend as quickly, but you learn to not sweat the small stuff.

I was lucky to stay healthy as I was moving up through the many football leagues I played in while growing up. Pure athleticism can even beat talent at times. I worked toward becoming a stronger man and better football player every step of the way. The stronger competition really elevated my level of play when I joined the Georgia Tech football team. It also increased the chance that my body was going to experience some new wear and tear under these intense conditions.

I saw an improvement in my football skills during my junior year at Georgia Tech. At the same time, I was beginning to experience a breakdown in my legs. A knee injury was going to set me back during my senior year and take me off the field completely. I wasn't thinking about the NFL draft, so in my heart, I really just wanted to play as many games for GT as possible, especially because I felt wanted.

Knowing my injury, the team still needed me to be involved in the last game of the season against our archrival Georgia. They had an all-American pass rusher who was a half sack away from setting his school record. This became my career focus for the moment.

My job was to shut down one of the country's top linebackers who was also projected to be a top-ranking defensive lineman in the next NFL draft. Sorry to say for him, he did not break the record that day.

Even though I was hurt, I pushed through the injury and completely shut him down. Something else happened to me on this day—something that I would not understand until I retired from my NFL career and sports all together.

The body is temporary. When there is something holding back an athlete from being 100 percent healthy, the athlete faces many demons emotionally. I felt inadequate as a competitor and felt like I was letting my team down.

You almost lose your inner purpose when you are not able to participate and help them get the win. You have spent so much in your life preparing for these moments, and then a break, sprain, or tear can wipe it away just like that.

A large population of kids rely on sports to advance in life, especially those coming from tough financial situations. There is a very low percentage of kids who make it to a paid or pro level. Despite that fact, kids in neighborhoods around the world still believe that they can do it—the exhausted and sweaty kids who are counting down the shot clock in their heads as they fade away, hitting the game-winning buzzer-beater. You know that you have done it before too.

They sit, dreaming about their families sitting on the couches next to them when the pro league commissioner calls out their name and putting on the hat of the team who wants to have them be a part of the franchises' winning future. They can feel the tears flowing while hugging Mom or Grandma, knowing they finally get the opportunity to move their family forward. Every practice, every ride, every knockdown, and every rise back up all lead up to that magical moment. Or not.

Most kids don't pay attention to their grades and only grind it out at practice with a stubborn and naive tunnel vision. When the time comes to hang up the cleats and they are not at a paid level, they rarely have a solid backup plan. A lot of kids turn to blue-collar work, and unfortunately, some turn to street work.

I was fortunate enough to make it to the pro level. Like they say, "More money, more problems." The higher up the ladder you go the higher the fall is physically, financially, and emotionally.

In football, every year you play is an extreme physical challenge, putting the body on the line again and again. Every day, every practice, and every play needs to be executed at 100 percent full speed. Even if your body is not ready, you make it ready because the next players are standing in line behind you, waiting for you to fall, like hungry hyenas.

Ironically, the locker room is the safest place for players; you are surrounded by your team and coaches, who are all working toward the same goal, spending every day developing and building up one another as a single unit. At the same time, we were building incredible trust as well. You might not agree on everything outside of football, but you trust each other.

Once you get the management involved, you are no longer a person; you are a number. Not the number on the back of the uniform you wear into battle day in and day out, but instead, you are one of the evil numbers that have dollar signs before them. They're always trying to get the best player for the best money.

It is a rare blessing to have a player walk away from the game healthy and willingly. If they can do that and they have some money tucked away, it might not get any better than that. When you're a nonprofessional player or on a practice squad, you are hoping to get your chance to earn a consistent role on the team. It only takes one wrong play to get hurt, and it could leave you with very few options in life.

I was twenty-three when I played in the National Football League and never planned for a future financially or emotionally if my career came to an end. The team offered additional player meetings and some guidance, but it did not feel genuine.

I was a twenty-three-year-old New Yorker and a fast-growing football celebrity. I did not trust where the information was coming from, nor did I take the time to research it beyond that. I was always out and about.

The league itself communicated with the players' union. So the union needed the league, and the league needed the cooperation of the players. The offices in between looked to benefit themselves and not the players as a whole.

Most of the time, you kept to yourself and walked your own path. I would go on to face my own hurdles when I left the NFL. Those hurdles turned out to be big ones that did not favor me as a person or player. I started to see the writing on the wall saying that my career was coming to a close.

A younger lineman was drafted before our Super Bowl run and received a handsome contract. Now, as a third-year veteran, I was fighting for a job against this fresh and dynamic athlete. I really needed to have knee surgery, but any skip in my step could take me off the roster for good. So of course, I played through it and tried to beat him out for the position.

The reality is that I should have been placed on the "injured reserve" with my place on the team held for me. That would not have made the front office, who selected the rookie look so well. To see that a hurt "hundred-thousand-aire" lineman was winning the practice battles was the last thing they wanted.

The team decided to keep me from playing. At the time, I felt I was the better player with my experience and strength. The powers that be fast-tracked the rookie to be out there and begin his career. In my opinion, they probably rushed him into the situation as well, which may have hurt his development in the long run.

Along with needing to heal, I should not have been practicing or participating in the games. The cost of war is often the warriors. I knew that the more the kid played, whether I was better than him or not, the further I would get pushed to the back burner.

The coaches asked me to dress for the big rivalry game against Chicago "just in case." At this point, I was really hiding my injury. There was so much going through my head on a daily basis. To play in the game could physically end my career even quicker, and to not play could do the same thing. I just waited, ready to see what my fate would be.

It was October 12, and the game was going to be a war. In one of the more back-and-forth contests in the rivalry, the Bears got off to a 10–0 lead. Alonzo Spellman hit the rookie I was competing with hard and took him out of the game early. You hate to see anyone go down in a game even if they are your direct competition. We are all still brothers in a tightly bound football family.

The kid really could have been good; he had the build and the skills. In my opinion, he just needed more time to develop instead of being forced to play. My number got called after the rookie was ruled out for the rest of the game. I made my choice to play for better or worse. I knew one thing was for sure: I was going to give it hell out there. And I did. We did.

I got to work, and our offense came back and took a 14–10 halftime lead. As the game was coming to a close, we escaped with a victory when the Bears missed a two-point conversion. We won but at a cost. I am sure I was not the only one out there who was playing hurt that day.

I made a conscious choice to play and seized the opportunity to battle—to do what I loved. We are often willing to sacrifice everything for true love, never thinking about the repercussions, consequences, or long-term effects but instead thinking about the hourglass resting on our souls.

Every fallen grain of sand within the hourglass is heavier than the last. We need to make the most of our time within ourselves so that when the hourglass has dropped its last stone, we would be wearing an eternal smile.

I went into that game and handled the job even though I should not have. That is life. I always maintained my respect with my teammates and within myself. It's more than that even.

I was a young Black man who clawed his way from the bottom of the pile to get to the highest stage in the sports world. The next generations of kids watch that closely. I put everything I had into it for the ones before me and the ones that will follow me next.

I was out of the rotation now. The team brought in a couple of veteran players to split duties with the rookie once his ankle healed, and that was how they finished out the season. Of course, I still dressed for every game, ready to play if they needed me.

After our Super Bowl season, my surgery happened, and I was not yet 100 percent. I was more like 50 percent. One day during practice, I was asked to come in for some drills to see how my knee held up. I was confused by this because I was still only at half capacity.

The coaches ignored my physical situation again instead of placing me on the injured reserve list. The purpose of the IR status is a mutual understanding to not run that player at full speed. At the same time, the team needed to get me the help I needed to recover from my injury. I limped through the drills as they filmed me. That was all the footage they needed. After that, it was the end of me.

Once word hits the front office about bad mobility and a possible career-ending injury, no one will touch you with a ten-foot pole. I was then released by the Packers, and so began the next chapters of my uncertain journey.

I could not let the way that my career ended tarnish all the positives that have come out of that experience. I would go on to play in other great leagues around the world and even the NFL again. It was about proving to everyone and myself that I could still compete at the highest level. Even more so, I needed to continue to do the best I could with whatever chance I got.

Tough times like those prepared me to overcome the next major obstacles in my uncertain life. The experiences left a reassurance in my heart that no matter what happens, I know that it all happens for a divine reason.

Everything will always work itself out with the right mindset. I continued to dig down deep inside myself, knowing that the strongest willpower can make it possible to live beyond our limitations. The body is temporary, but the mind is forever. Do the best you can with what you have.

Chapter 9

FATHER KNOWS BEST

It's as if when the key hit the doorknob, the smell of fresh breakfast off the griddle filled the air. My father was always the first one to arrive at work and the last one to leave the restaurant. His pride is behind his work and his family name to this day. If you wanted to enjoy some of the meanest grits on Long Island, you were absolutely coming to my father's place: Brown's Best Country Kitchen.

That man ran a restaurant during a time when it was not so easy to do that. He was also doing it in a neighborhood that was not the safest or most desirable. That being said, our family remembers him going in and running it day in and day out without ever complaining. He was one of the hardest-working people I've ever met in my life. I could not have asked for a stronger example of what a man should be like growing up. The saying "Be humble and work hard" was in front of us in everything we did as kids.

You have to be very dedicated when representing your own business and your own brand. When the flow is good and the money is good, it's easy to forget what it took to get there. It's also hard to see the reality that you will be the one marked if it fails. You will always be judged by your last move or decision in this world.

I carried this with me in my football career. I moved forward with my family's fundamentals as well as my own learned work ethic. I was willing to do what it took to win as a team. At times, that meant playing backup, and other times, it meant being the starter.

It feels different taking the field as a starter as opposed to playing the backup role. You walk differently, talk differently, and certainly act differently.

I had been striving to fulfill my dream of playing in the NFL. Once I was drafted by the Steelers and traded to the Packers, that all became a reality.

We were entering the year where we would go on to win the Super Bowl. I had a good rookie year and was projected to become a starter if I kept progressing at the rate that I was. I finally got my opportunity to do so. On the field, that meant you were the best of the best. You were looked up to by your teammates with respect. At the same time, you were getting looks of hunger as they tried to take that position for themselves.

Also, being at the top of the food chain puts a target on your back. The NFL is a cutthroat business. There are always three people waiting and wanting to take your job. I know because I was one of them. I was put in the driver's seat now for the offensive line and fed off of it.

Starting for the Packers changed my life all around. Being a starter on other teams sure had its benefits, but starting in Green Bay was like becoming a green god. That power swells you from head to toe. My muscles felt bigger, and so did my ego. Confidence, like anything in life, is only good in moderation.

I was feeding into that part of my life more than my earlier foundations, which my father taught me. My social schedule started to get as big as my biceps. When you're a backup, it is like being lost in a *Where's Waldo* book.

When you're a starter, you are recognized by the community as a top player. This Packers community makes you feel like it's the height of any fame. Your name is in the papers, the bulletins, and the news. With fame comes responsibility.

When you start to fly, you forget what it's like to have your feet on the ground. I was starting to forget myself. I had a teammate who left the NFL to go play in NFL Europe during our season. He was a really big kid, young and strong. We were good friends on the team.

Coincidentally, he was also from Long Island. When he came back from that European experience, I was at my peak. I was the starting left tackle for the Packers and rolling strong.

The locker room is like a family living room, a comedy club, and a principal's office all in one. It's a place where teammates share the most intimate details, arguments, and bonds. When my teammate returned home from NFL Europe, he was different.

He had lost all this weight, he felt he lost his competitive edge, and he was very depressed. He was complaining that the food was terrible, the people were strange, and the football playing experience was nothing like what it was here.

I am not a bully, and I never was. On this day, I was not hearing my friend's story with sympathetic ears. Instead, I was taking it in with a poor sense of pride. I immediately reacted to his story by putting him down. "Are you crazy? I would never go play there!" I ranted. "I would quit football before I ever did that."

I think part of me was also afraid inside to have to travel somewhere far like that. I was twenty-five years old. When you come from Brentwood, Long Island, kids don't just up and go to places like Europe. We just didn't do it, nor could we afford to do it.

Mix that with my fear of losing my job, and it kept pushing these negative remarks out of me. I was just slaying him with blinders on. After all, I was protecting future Hall of Famer Brett Favre and projected to do so throughout this year and next year.

It's funny how life works out. A full circle completes any lesson. No more than a year later after that incident in the locker room, so much had happened. We had won a Super Bowl, and I was up for knee surgery. I was fighting to even be considered for the team roster for the following year.

Green Bay chose a left tackle as their number 1 pick the year before. Now I had youth chomping at my heels while I was fighting through a tough injury. The same coaches who had encouraging voices when I was healthy were now in the process of gently letting me down.

"Don't worry, Gary, we will wait for you to get healthy," they said from the corners of their mouths.

They were only out to protect their new investments and themselves. The players in the end are only tools in a bigger game. I was suddenly sent out onto the practice field to perform a drill. I questioned why I did not have a red pinnie on to symbolize an injured player. They told me I didn't need one, which was wrong because I was hurt.

But again, I was in a game where you have to fight no matter what to keep your job, so I begrudgingly went out there to perform the drill to the best of my ability. I was at half speed at best with the injury, and they had the cameras rolling.

Now they had me practicing on film, looking my worst. This was all the team needed to cut me. Just like that, I was done. One day, I was the man, and the next day, I was unemployed with no backup plan.

I found myself sitting back in my childhood room in my mom's house. Like any mother, the photos and memories were still as I left them. She may have shuffled them around slightly to do some dusting, but everything was still there. I sat and looked at the pictures, just in awe that at one time, I fantasized about being one of those sports players or those musical artists.

It was the only thing that mattered in my young heart. You would give anything to have it. Then I earned the opportunity and lost it in the same breath. Don't get me wrong. I was so blessed for all I accomplished in my career leading up to becoming a champion. It was incredible! Once I realized it was all over, it hit me like a ton of bricks. I did not know anything besides football, and I had to get back somehow.

Ironically, I was trying out for the Barcelona Dragons, a team playing in the NFL European League—the same league my teammate played in when I howled that I would rather die before playing in that league.

Now, I thought I would die if I didn't play for them. I still couldn't believe that just behind me was a life where I had motorcycles, all the friends I wanted, and NFL money. I was playing football at the highest level.

I tried to keep busy working while I was trying out and hoping to revive my football career. I was obsessed with getting a job one way or another. Everywhere I applied to was telling me I was overqualified for the labor, and they wouldn't hire me. I was confused and started to panic.

It had not entered my mind because I was in a successful place playing football, but where I come from, there were people making more money than I did. They were doing it by conducting illegal work. In life's low moments, it is easy to forget the examples that got you where you are. I started to sway to the dark side and think, *Well, I am from here. Maybe I should just hustle here too.* No money, no job, and a slipping sense of self-worth pave an easy way into that game of depression.

I never heard from the coaches after the European draft. That was all it took, and I gave up hope. I was going to make a tough choice and stick to it. I left my room, walked past my father, and left my house to hit the street. I had a guy I knew who moved "big weight" on the island. I brought what money I had left and stocked up on some product. Getting it was one thing. Knowing where to push it was another. I headed to a local bar where people would hustle. I sat down, started to put back some Jack Daniels, and waited.

At home, my father was there to intercept a call that should have gotten through that morning. The coaching staff for the Dragons was wrapping up their draft day, and the two coaches thought one or the other had called me. Upon realizing this, they reached out again and got my father. I made the team as the number 1 draft pick. Now my father had to find a way to tell me.

Back at the bar, I finally found two customers. These guys were asking if I knew where to get some product. I told them to meet me in the bathroom in ten minutes. I threw back one more shot, got up, and got ready to make my first deal. While I was waiting in the bathroom, my phone rang. It was my father.

It's funny how a parent knows so much about their children by the slump of a shoulder, a slip in a walk, or an uneasy demeanor. He was worried about me from the moment I left. He told me there was just something in my face that haunted him from the moment I walked out the door. The look in my eyes said it all.

He told me that coaches had made a communication error and finally got through to our house with the news that I was the first draft pick for the Barcelona Dragons. I made the team. He told me he didn't want me doing anything stupid and to get right back home. I hesitated for a moment, almost committing to making the deal anyway. At the last minute, I backed out and left the bar.

There are a number of times that my career and life were almost over. This was definitely one of those moments. It turned out that after I left the bar, they raided it. The two men who were going to come back into the bathroom and meet me were undercover cops. In a split second, I would have gone from Super Bowl Champion to Brentwood's busted drug kingpin on a single deal.

How many other kids are in that same situation but do not have the family support to back out, even at the last minute? I would have become another statistic, another Black male doing what "other Black males" end up doing. Thank God my father is the man he is and made me the man I am today.

I was still broke and had this useless product now. I went back to the dealer who was a friend of mine and asked for a favor that is usually never ever given. I asked for my money back. It's not like there is a receipt for this stuff. By divine intervention, his heart was softened. He said that because of who I was, he would take back what I bought and give me back the cash. I got lucky again.

I decided to go and play for Barcelona, the place I once mocked in that locker room. Not only did I go and play there, but I loved it. I was so thankful to be playing football again. It also didn't hurt that my hotel was right near a nude beach. The weather was beautiful, and the wind was finally back in my sails. I was inches away from sitting in jail instead of strapping on the pads again.

"Stay humble, do what's right, and work hard." I strayed from my father's words, and it almost ended my career and maybe my life. Listen to those who care about you even if you think you know better. It could save you too.

En esta página, Judith, rodeada de dragones, luce un traje sastre de falda tubo y chaqueta corta con manga tres cuartos, en seda salvaje rosa chicle, de Lydia Delgado. Reloj con correa rosa, en acero, de Boucheron. Zuecos de charol, de Pura López.

A la derecha, Judith lleva un vestido de corte lencero, con sujetador incorporado, en rayón elástico, de D & G de Dolce & Gabbana.

LA BELLA Y LAS 'BESTIAS'

Judith Mascó POSA EN ESTE REPORTAJE CON EL MEJOR EQUIPO DE FÚTBOL AMERI-CANO DE EUROPA. LA MODELO ESPAÑOLA SE DIVIRTIÓ JUGANDO *con los 'dragones'.*

FOTOGRAFÍA: ARTUR LLEÓ / ESTILISMO: ANNA VALLÉS

Chapter 10

NEVER SAY *NEVER*

A knee injury that would not go away played a part in my career winding down during my Canadian football experience. I was still better than other lineman even when I was hurt, but football is a strange business.

However, that's life, and I was back home on Long Island in my mother's house, in my old room, recovering from what would be the last of my football-related surgeries. In my head, I was still the professional football player on the world's highest stage. I was Super Bowl champion Gary Brown, and everyone knew it.

I was working four jobs to keep up with the financial demands that come with being a local celebrity, like walking into a bar and everyone expecting you to pick up the tab—things like that. I was constantly signing autographs and taking pictures with people.

Hell, when I was trying to apply for jobs, the interviewers would tell me I was overqualified for the work but still had the nerve to ask for a signed photo.

I didn't care that I might have been overqualified. I just needed the money. I was still big and strong, so I found myself doing hands-on gigs. I was working security, running clubs, doing custodial work, and managing construction crews. We grew up in a blue-collar household, so these were just new ways of making a living. However, the reasons for which I was working were not healthy for me, and the pace was feverish.

At one of my maintenance jobs, I went from wearing a Super Bowl ring to scrubbing toilets and was damn good at it. I took pride in everything I ever did and always earned everything I ever wanted.

I worked my way up the ladder and was soon managing that building. One day, we had an unexpected gas leak and needed to clear the place. We began to do our emergency evacuation of everyone in the facility. There was a woman who was not able to get from the third floor to the exterior with the elevators shut down, so we had to use the stairs.

This woman was battling dementia and could feel the tension in the air. When my team entered her apartment in a chaotic rush, she did not know how to react.

I redirected my crew to continue clearing the floor and personally carried her down to safety. I was someone she recognized and trusted despite her panic during the situation.

I was in top shape, and carrying her was nothing. I can still hear the sirens roaring in the background. My mind was running through all the checkpoints in my head, making sure we did not miss anyone in the building. We safely and successfully got everyone out; however, during that walk down the stairs, I hurt my lower back.

As a big, tough guy, naturally, I rubbed some dirt on it and kept going about my daily life. In reality, I was seriously injured and could not predict what was coming next.

I herniated my T10 and T11 disks in my thoracic spine. Basically, the bone was putting intense pressure on my spine. Although I was able to continue to walk and be mobile with this injury at first, a monster would rear its ugly head in the coming months.

All of a sudden, I found myself lifeless from the waist down just like that. You can't even imagine processing looking down at two legs that once stomped on NFL playing fields and not having them not look back at you. The little things hit first. I was living alone at the time and needed to go to the bathroom.

At the time, I was almost four hundred pounds and out of shape. I was paralyzed but still stubborn. Who else was going to get me there? To think I may never walk again and that this was what life was going to look like was very depressing, almost life-threatening.

I was panting and crying to myself as I made my way to the toilet. I rolled off the bed and began.

I moved my weathered elbows forward one at a time, pinning them to the floor like ice picks penetrating a steep mountain face. Toxic sweat ran freely from my throbbing forehead. I was cursing and praying while pulling my upper body in a rhythmic pace to guide my stomach across the filthy bedroom floor.

The torturous journey seemed to extend for miles. Completely exhausted, I dragged my lifeless legs as a tractor would while pulling two rusty sickles through stiff dirt. Reality had set in hard. Worst of all, when I was finished, I had to get back to the bed. Something had to be done.

I landed at Dr. Daniel Brandenstein's office, where things would take a turn. I wouldn't let anyone see me in my current state, so my parents and my girlfriend did everything for me. They were the only ones I could be around, and that was even tough for me. I always worried I was more of a burden than a blessing. Dr. Brandenstein ordered some scans on my spine. The results put us all on high alert.

He sent me straight to the ER for surgery. I did grab some food on our way across the street because I had not eaten. I looked at it as my last supper before going under the knife. A steak and glass of wine would have been better, but the fast-food joint near the hospital was on the menu for tonight.

Life was over as I knew it. I would now look at the world in such a different light. I was prepared to go under the knife for better or worse. It was time.

Leading up to the surgery, my conditions were getting worse, and they were taking forever diagnosing me. It's all about the dollars and often comes at the high cost of people's livelihoods.

To be honest, it was more than the slow-moving system. I was also afraid to get the surgery. It wasn't even planned. The stubborn athlete in me thought I could beat my injury on my own. They had not yet diagnosed me, so how could they fully know what they were doing with my body? I lost my feeling from the waist down because they did not catch the real issue in the initial assessments.

As soon as I got in the ER, it was go time. This procedure was not just being done to possibly save my mobility. We were doing it to prevent the injury from causing a full-body paralysis. We needed to perform surgery on two herniated disks: my T10 and T11 thoracic spine.

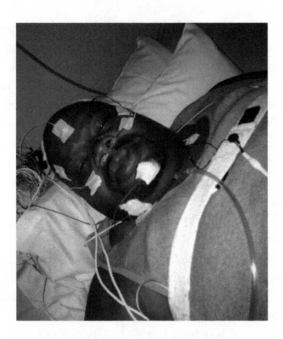

If you pinch a nerve and pull it right off, there is not too much damage to the body. If the nerve stays pinched, then it will rarely grow back. The extended time period between the injury and the surgery is one of the main factors in possibly never being able to walk again. I was mentally planning on the worst-case scenario as part of my new reality, but I had to survive the night first.

It was almost like falling asleep during the most important movie of my life. The rolling, rhythmic beeps of my lifeline slowly pulsed across the monitor. Strangers behind masks and fogged glasses murmured to one another, sidestepping around my large frame and huffing procedural orders to one another as they took me apart. I faded.

Think back to being a kid and that nostalgic sound of kicking a can full of rocks. Imagine that: being happy with nothing but your friends while running around, kicking a can. There is a carefree joy that comes with movement. We feel it when we skip, run, or simply walk around. I hoped I would find that innocence again from my wheelchair.

There were aspects of the surgery that would extend the operating time. I was a very large man, and Dr. B said that the part of my chest they had to access was over a foot deep into my body. Finding difficulty going from the front, they had to switch gears and go from the side. They were prepared for this and began navigating through the detour. Dr. B and his team moved like music, not thinking about the time but instead, the perfect process.

They filleted me open like a trophy shark on a sunny Long Island dock. Finally, after meticulously deflating a lung and removing a rib, they were able to access my spinal column. My family was panicking. My mother was a nurse and thought I should have been done by now.

A lot of times, people are so focused on the person in trouble that they forget about the people in their support group. The emotional supportive weight that they carry is incredible. I always struggled with people coming in to see me and then leaving the room crying. They could not help but feel sorry for me, and that was a difficult relationship to process at the time.

I give my girl all the credit in the world. When all of this was happening, I had a hard conversation with her about what "we" would look like in the future. I was chair-ridden. That might be as good as I could get, and there was a chance I could get worse.

I was having anxiety about her quality of life because of my current state. This was putting me down even further because now I was confronting something that had not even happened yet, and I was willing to let it all go to avoid embarrassment or inconvenience. It's important to know that oftentimes, the people with the scars from these life situations are not always the one with the injuries.

I remember sitting there, somehow okay with losing her because I did not believe in my new self. I was wrong. With a stern look and raised eyebrow, she made it clear she was not going anywhere.

"Gary, we could live in a cardboard box for the rest of our lives, and I would not care. I am not going anywhere," she verbally cemented. From then on, we were rolling together as one.

Whenever I do charity work in the hospital now, I always seek out the friends and family of the patient. I make sure they are included and recognized. You never know until you know. Support is so important in all phases of life, especially traumatic ones like this.

The surgery was finally done, and I was in the recovery unit, waiting for my girl and my family to come see me. The machines beeped like an orchestra playing songs off the new soundtrack of my life. I lay there with half my face swollen with blood and the other half a skeleton drained dry. It was a similar image in my heart. I was half alive and half dead. I was so sad, needing help and not sure how to ask for it.

Your pride is an interesting power. When everything is clicking in a forward direction in life, positive pride can bring you to the very top. When you are at rock bottom, it can become your worst enemy. When it completely turns on you and becomes embarrassment, there lies another layer of adversity stronger than magic. It was one of the many nuances that were part of my new life as one who was paralyzed.

It was now a week after my surgery. I was confused and in constant pain, hooked up to stomach tubes and relying on the hospital to stay alive. It all added up to a very difficult challenge of staying focused on healing and having a positive mentality.

I would have plenty of time in the hospital to continue this journey. Something was holding me back from moving forward with my healing both physically and mentally. Time was just passing by, and I felt like I was just standing still.

That year, it was a bitter cold December on Long Island. The recovery room I was in felt so hot to me even though everyone else insisted it was normal. As the snow softly fell outside the hospital room window, I was burning up inside.

They had six large ice packs strapped to me like roller derby pads. They kept refreshing them over and over again to keep my temperature down. There was a revolving team of amazing nurses caring for me.

In the middle of the night, a new nurse came in to check on me. She was a sweet Haitian woman and fearlessly strutted in. Her bright smile was strong enough to bring light into my dark, depressing room.

She sat, stroking my forehead with a cold rag as if she was painting my mind a new picture. She softly sympathized with me, saying, "I see big, strong men like you all the time, fighting so hard. Just let go of it, baby. You don't have to hold it in. Just let go." She may have been talking to my spirit, but my body started to listen. I faded.

The next thing I recall is waking up to a violent internal heave. My body was rejecting blood from my lungs. The dried-up crimson cinder became free as it splattered on the floor.

This graphic event marked the moment my body started to heal. A surreal sense of calm soothed my mind. My temperature came down, and the room felt comfortable again. I felt comfortable again.

Everything started to seem better. If I had a chocolate pudding, it would have even tasted better! It appeared I was moving on to the next level, the one that would test the mind as much as it has tested the body. I did not know if I was ready for it, nor did I have a choice.

Once I was fully awake, I wanted to thank her for helping me. I hailed down every nurse and was asking if she could come back to see me. The staff repeatedly informed me there was no one who worked there that fit that description. I insisted on it, describing her uniform, accent, and comforting activity with me. I didn't believe them and kept asking anyone who came in.

Sometimes angels show up when they are needed most. They always leave a little something behind in our hearts that we can use to pass on to someone else: a sense of calm during the wildest storms and a little mystery to keep us wondering. She may have never been seen again, but she will always be real to me.

There was a man in the recovery room with me that week who was not doing so well with coming to terms with his injury. He lost his leg during a motorcycle accident and was still very upset. He had a lot of anger, understandable guilt, anxiety, and confusion.

I would try and tell him it was going to be okay; however, it fell on deaf and nearly defeated ears. He pleaded with the Lord, wishing the accident had killed him, saying that he could not live like this.

There are very real and hard emotions to compartmentalize during the time of trauma. I think as much as I annoyed him with positive banter, some of it had to break through. I made it clear I was going to ask him how he was doing every day. He promised me he would never say he was doing well even if he was.

Despite his coldness to me, I was up for the challenge. In a way, it actually helped me take my mind off my current state. When you are going through something like this, an idle mind can be a dangerous one. We need to put our problems aside and dedicate ourselves to serving others. That act has a greater power than we could ever imagine.

While he was wishing his life was over, I got busy on how I was going to adapt. Always lead by example. I tried not to have a pity party during this. I could have blamed others during the process, but that was not going to make me walk again. My willpower was going to do that. I continued on in physical therapy, making progress on what seemed an impossible feat: walking again.

A few months later, after leaving therapy one day, I ran into him by sheer chance. When he saw me, he popped a wheelie in his chair. His face lit up with a genuine smile stretching from ear to ear. He did it. He overcame the emotional hump that seemed impossible to him. He was alive again within himself.

I felt good that I was there at the beginning, giving him positive food for thought. I am not saying I saved his life, but I proved to myself that attitude is everything. If we can provide positive reassurance for one another, it all adds up in a good way. I truly believe the world will be a better place if we take the time to do that in daily practice.

We are all part of a team—from the doctors to the families to the patients. Dr. B and his amazing staff did their jobs medically. It was up to me and my family after that to do our job next. We needed to heal together both inside and out.

I constantly push myself so that I may one day walk upright again. It starts off with getting your feet on the floor then staring at your foot, trying to wiggle your toes. Then comes holding yourself upright until eventually you can drag your feet with a walker. Next comes turning the drag into a slide and eventually a stride.

Having it actually happen is a real miracle. I am blessed with the ability to use my experience to share with others. It is important that they do not feel alone during those moments like I did while crawling on my stomach across the floor—the dark nights where you find yourself crying out to God, begging the question "Why me?"

I still see all the doctors and staff for regular checkups. My autographed photo hangs in their office lobby. Turns out, Dr. B is an avid fisherman. Like all of us fishermen, he gets anxious during the winter months, waiting for the break of spring. Dr. B busies himself making custom fishing poles during this time. He gifts them to family members and keeps a couple for himself.

He fashioned a rod in my favorite colors and in a unique style and gifted it to me. It is awesome! I have been doing some great fishing with it. Even more so, I have been doing some great living with it. I am blessed with the abilities that I have and try to use them to the fullest. Just because you may never walk again does not mean you will never live again. You cannot forget that.

Dr. B says after all his surgeries, his greatest feelings come from seeing his patients gain their independence again. It does not always mean walking again but working toward living life at the greatest level possible for each individual. Seeing them gain spiritual independence is just as glorious as physical independence. No matter what your situation is, you have the ability and willpower to achieve your individual life goals. You have to focus on it with everything you have as if your life depends on it. You will find out from time to time that it does.

Chapter 11

Rock Bottom

I was trying to adjust to life without using my legs. You take a lot for granted until it's taken from you. The simple acts of getting up to use the restroom, reaching a tall cabinet, or running to the mailbox happen so routinely that you rarely think about what it would be like if you could not do those things for yourself anymore.

I started feeling self-conscious about being in public with a wheelchair, walker, or cane. There was a very difficult transition of processing how people once viewed me and how they see me now. You reflect inward and try to find ways in which you are still special.

It is a lot of hard work to love the person you are no matter what. Regardless, it did not make life outside of my house any easier. I started looking at some events that were coming up and thinking of how I was going to approach them as the new Gary.

I really didn't even want to leave the house. But my sister was going to get married, and her wedding was approaching. I remember wanting nothing more than to walk her down the aisle myself or at least be there to witness it myself. I had no idea what options I would have with my new body.

Before the wedding, we worked on getting me ready. It took three hours to dress me with all my family's help. In some stories, the wedding party is busy with champagne toasting with smiles on and a sparkle in the air. In our room, three people were dripping with sweat as they put on my final garments. They themselves had to get ready again after the effort from sweating so badly. I was a big man with a lifeless lower half.

I don't even remember the wedding. I was flooded with pain, embarrassment, and physical discomfort. As soon as it was over, I got the hell out of there.

I was so excited and determined to attend. I had no idea it would turn out like it did. During the months leading up to the wedding, simply attending was a goal that motivated me during the therapies.

The harsh realization that life had changed was setting in. I needed several people to dress me and to help me down the aisle on her special day. I was supposed to be carrying her. I was starting to understand I was never going to be the same Gary again, and I began to decline throughout my mind, body, and soul.

I was fresh off a successful football career. I was broke and now paralyzed. Mentally, there was a lot going on inside. I was experiencing so much frustration from knowing that on the outside, I was physically capable of doing so much but that inside, there was an unseen injury that was holding me back from doing it.

When the injury fully unfolded, I lost all feeling from the waist down. I could not work or walk. I needed full care. I was begrudgingly being helped by nurses and medical staff. The first thing that goes in that situation is your pride. Having someone else wiping your behind for you was just the beginning of this horrible journey.

I befriended this nice guy in the ER who was big and strong. He was part of the man power team, as they called it. When they would come and move me from bed to bed, I'd ask if they would move my legs and let them touch the ground.

I asked if they could come every chance they were available to do it. They obliged and helped me again and again. It was a far reach for normalcy but really helped me mentally. In the back of your head, you still believe you can walk again one day, or at least I was hoping like hell.

I moved to a rehab center where they pursued this possibility of walking again. Despite the extreme efforts, I still came home in a wheelchair. It would be later that year that we would discover feelings in my legs. However, with getting feeling back also came the pain.

Pain is still something I deal with today, but when it started out, it was new and eye-opening. Being paralyzed clearly damaged my mobility and was starting to bring on mental anguish.

Eventually, when the feeling came back, mobility with pain was worse. It was my terrible tax to keep moving toward a life I once knew. Before I would begin moving, I would have to come face-to-face with death. As crazy as it sounds, it was a step in the right direction.

On the outside, I tried to be happy-go-lucky. I tried to hide what was happening inside because of who I was before my injury. It's when you are alone at night that self-pity consumes you. Tear-filled rants fell on deaf ears. "Why me? What did I do wrong? Who am I?"

Once I returned home from surgery, it was to my place, which I had started to demolish before injuring my spine. It was a dark place to be physically and mentally. The walls were ripped out, and there were very little to no amenities. There wasn't even a knob on the door, only a padlock hanging on a rusty bracket.

The frustrating part was I couldn't do anything about any of it. Not only was I still broke, but I had no way of making money. Everything I have ever done was with my hands and feet. It was not going well.

There is one thing that you can do while just sitting there, and that's drink. I was finding myself slipping lower and lower into the bottle. I had a higher tolerance than most people because of my size. A shot is like a glass of water to me. The most dangerous factor was losing hope within myself. The drinks go down a lot quicker than you think when hope leaves the room.

That's the devastating part about being at the bottom, and I mean the rock bottom. You think you might be there, but you're not sure. You don't think it can get any worse, nor do you care if it does. All your values, morals, and safeguards drop. You no longer listen to the "inner voice," the voice that once guided you to positive places, victories, and most importantly…love.

I stopped loving life, and worst yet, I stopped loving myself. Well, maybe I just didn't start loving my new self. It was easy to love the old me—the champ, the athletic freak of nature. The new me was yet to be discovered.

One morning, I started it like the rest. I consumed a handful of pain pills for my back. I was in a dreamlike state and lay back down to slip into another uncomfortable sleep. I was startled by a phone call from a friend who told me he was on his way over.

I knew what that meant: we were going to be chilling. Unfortunately, I forgot I had woken up once already. I took the same handful of prescription pills and then waited for my friend to arrive. Upon arrival, we lit up a cigar and made a couple of drinks before I even had breakfast.

The type of pain pills I was taking were of the highest potency and caliber. This did not help my current situation. Everything caught up to me, and I could not escape the dreadful wave.

There is a moment of fading light when you turn off life's lamp. A short mysterious journey had me fading helplessly further from the actual light.

My friend saw me become unplugged and going down. I stuttered with slow lips to call my brother, who just happened to be in town. When he arrived, he checked my pulse and called the paramedics immediately.

Somehow I knew I needed the ambulance, but pride and fear got in my way along with the impact from the drugs. I hoped my brother would either be able to save me himself or force me to get the help I needed. I overdosed.

The paramedics arrived and began to revive me. As I was coming back to reality, I heard them joking about a photo of myself with Bill Clinton at Lambeau Field I had sitting out. He paid us a visit during the season before we went on to be Super Bowl champions.

That's one of many incredible memories I was letting slip away instead of appreciating for the time they existed in my blessed life.

Now these men that were saving my life were laughing at the photo and me. They kept mocking it as if it was staged or fake.

How could that strong, upright man shaking hands with the president of the United States be the same person who nearly slipped away from this planet this morning? All four men carried me out of the house on a stretcher.

I was revived and given the care I needed to continue to live. I believe I did die that day, the other me—the one that had no hope and no desire to love and appreciate life. I was dead alive. A new me was going to come back to start a new life.

There was no hiding. I had a big problem, and I had to do something about it—but not alone. I had my family and some real friends who would begin helping me through this and helping me restore my will to rise above.

My routine at home changed, and my eyes were opened to the world as well as my desire to get well. I was inspired one evening watching a quadriplegic-turned-motivational speaker onstage named Nick Vujicic.

Here he was telling thousands of able-bodied people how to live. Imagine that. I don't remember how, but I know it happened instantly. I was on the phone with Big Brothers Big Sisters, signing up to mentor one of their youth members. It was my time to give back.

I stopped feeling sorry for myself and started putting my energy into helping others. When you shut down the pity party, it opens up a lot of room for positive energy that can be spread to everyone else you meet, especially others in need.

Although it did not look like I was going to fight back, at the final hour, I was given a second chance. My name was on the darkest list for a quick instant, but I didn't give in. I moved to the next stage in my recovery. I grabbed it by the horns and took control.

I started looking at my situation not as a curse but instead as a blessing. There are others out there that can benefit from the ugly details of that struggle that I went through—real people who could benefit from the moment I chose to climb back up on my feet. I was back in the fight to stay on the team called life not just for myself but for every person I can help moving forward.

Chapter 12

WHEN THE SWEAT DRIES

Autograph. Something written or made with one's own hand, an original manuscript or work of art, a person's handwritten signature, something that cannot be duplicated (Merriam-Webster's Dictionary).

An autograph signing is a fascinating and powerful interaction. Something special happens when someone eagerly seeks a specific figure out of appreciation and admiration. This can range from presidents, movie stars, artists, authors, and of course, sports figures.

Beyond the financial aspects of the memorabilia business, there is an emotional connection between the fan and the figure. There are levels to that interaction. Some people find that joy by being at the event, getting a signature, or even interacting live with the figure. All these forms of appreciation are so humbling.

When I first left the NFL, I was approached about writing a book. I was a young adult on a downward spiral while sitting in my childhood room at my mom's house. I stared at the floor between my feet and thought the only title that my book could have was "When Nobody Wants Your Autograph Anymore" or "When the Crowd Stops Cheering."

Shoot, when you put my name into Google, it only showed all my bad news, all the negative articles from my youthful mistakes. I needed to shift that energy desperately because too often was I emotionally down when I searched within myself. Depression was dominating my psyche, and the feeling that fame was slipping away from me or was almost completely gone was very difficult to deal with.

I was trying to keep up the image of the Super Bowl champ. It became routine for me to take the hundred bucks in my pocket and spend eighty of it at the bar, buying strangers and fake friends drinks. Meanwhile, I really needed that money to put toward my stack of bills.

Fame is as much of a drug as any of the physical substances out there. I was holding on to something that was dragging me deeper and deeper into the depths of depression. I needed to let go as soon as I could, and eventually, I did.

I am writing a book now because I realize that there is so much life to live. Back then in my own head, my life was over. It took a lot to get over that hump, and a lot of this book reflects on those struggles and challenges that led up to me being able to start a new life while preserving my heralded past as a professional athlete.

Signing something for someone gives me a strange sense of purpose and is one that is greatly appreciated. I still love doing autograph sessions when I get the chance, and I am always grateful for every day that someone still asks for my autograph.

In the definition, it says that an autograph cannot be duplicated. This also serves true for the life of the person signing the autograph. When the weight of the pen hits the paper, it is not just scribing a name. It is pushing the pen to create a visual of who that person is at that exact moment.

A culmination of life experiences all leading up to that very point on the blue plume scribing my name says it all. The balance within comes from being proud of that name being written on a daily basis.

When that era ends for a public figure, there are a lot of emotions and situations that arise. You spend so much time looking back at the moments that made you feel important, and these are the moments that gave you purpose at that time in your life. For me, during that time, I appreciated the ride of my sports career so much. But as they say, "all good things must come to an end."

As an athlete, I played the game every day out of pure love for the sport. I focused on winning at that moment. It took effort to never get too far ahead of myself. I really needed to reflect on that mindset after football while I was trying to start a new life and while overcoming many physical and mental obstacles.

In this book, I have spoken about many of those situations after my career. Depression, paralysis, and financial struggle were all there for me after my time as an athlete. All these things surrounded me while I was trying to figure out what I was going to do and who I was going to become. I discovered that giving back to my community was going to be my tool to help heal myself and those around me.

When I was playing football, there was always something else going on when I came across volunteering opportunities. As a celebrity at that time in my life, a party sounded a lot more attractive than scooping food for the homeless.

I wasn't a bad person, but communal problems aren't truly understood until you need that same help yourself. Once something impacts you directly, then you realize how important volunteering is in balancing your life and soul.

I missed my team, my teammates, and my purpose. I missed all the people that I had a unique bond with from all those years. The reality was that I was struggling so badly and almost dead inside.

I had sat on the highest sports stage in the world, and now I was back home in my mama's house—right where I started. I hit the absolute bottom. It was not until I discovered the power of giving back that my life started to change for the better. I was welcomed into places and circles, but I still always felt alone.

Now my heart is so happy from the fulfilment I get from all my philanthropy work. I am constantly making friends through sharing my experience with people who take the time to listen and the people who really need to hear it that day. I know how delicate life is because I've seen how quickly it can be taken away.

I am constantly focusing on my journey forward in life. I try daily to leave the football player switch off and the "new" Gary Brown switch on. It's tough. Up until recently, I've had a hard time with that. Then I started working with transitioning veterans. The military community has really helped me in my healing process.

I dedicate a lot of time to our veterans, working with a group called Play for Your Freedom. I have been working with them since day 1—January 28, 2016, to be exact. We help provide wellness workshops for veterans and their families using fitness and peer-to-peer support.

It's a true joy to be able to get back on the field again, playing and coaching with the service members and their families. It gives me such an amazing sense of purpose, belonging to a peer group that has also lost their teams, units, and oftentimes so much more.

There is a strong connection between the military community and the football community. Obviously, one is with guns while one involves a football, but the foundational principles align. You get your team, I'll get mine, and we will see who wins this strategic and physical battle. We become a collection of energy working together and forming an unbreakable bond.

When your time is up and the teams are gone, you are left fighting alone. When I am working with the military community, I contribute to a group effort in providing an atmosphere where they can find that team again, a place where they can build similar relationships with others seeking to heal and transition to a "normal" life.

I feel such a sense of belonging when I am with them. They gave so much so that I could live a free life, play sports, and enjoy myself. For me, I experience such a sense of honor and pride to offer them a photo with my signature on it at the end of our workshops.

It's powerful to share a bond with them. We work through our issues together using sports and friendship. It's as much for me as it is for them, and we all benefit from that unified connection with one another.

We don't have to fight alone anymore. I always remind them to band together again because only a veteran knows what a veteran has been through. It's the same thing with my fellow alumni. That post-career or service transition is so important. It needs to be positive in all aspects of your life. In a split second, it can easily be filled with self-medication and self-harm.

I still have tough days, but this work helps me through those days, the days where my injuries rear their ugly heads. Lack of sleep, disabled body parts, and permanent ache are few. Volunteering gets me out of bed, knowing that someone else is counting on me to show up and share my story so that together, we can create hope.

I always say, "I can either hurt at home or hurt here with you." There is a great appreciation for showing up to these meetings no matter what. After all, who more than our United States veterans show up when we need them the most?

At one point in time, I let the label of Super Bowl champ define me. Now, when we do our motivational talks in the hospitals, I am initially welcomed into the units as a former player and Super Bowl champ. Once we get into the community work and deliver the positive message about hope, we all realize we are there for the same reasons.

I am no longer just a sports figure to them but instead, a peer and ally in the fight to heal, which is a fight that cannot be taken on alone, as I have learned. It's a fight that starts within our hearts.

It took a lot for me to see the value in giving back. Like I said, when you're working hard, you're playing hard. When you are alone and know that deep down inside, you still have something to offer, you start to think differently. Your eyes become aware and more open to understand these opportunities to serve others.

Attitude is everything. It is not just about the money, large crowds, or big events. It is about how you treat someone you meet in the grocery store or on the street and when you actually take the time to look someone in the eyes and connect with them.

Being handicapped changed my life in so many ways. First, I lost my job as an athlete, and then I lost the means to physically earn a living. I did not know when the downward fall was going to stop.

It added a very heavy layer of complication to my life. These events hurt my identity and magnified my mental health struggles—all the more reason I am able to connect with people who struggle within.

Every time I am able to personally connect with someone and try to brighten their day, I make sure to let them know with great appreciation that it does the same thing to me.

I have spent so much time rebuilding my character. I slowly gained confidence by accepting who and where I was in life. I turned into Superman the day I stopped caring if people saw I was handicapped.

I didn't care anymore if they saw me using a cane, a wheelchair, or a walker. I am a better person now for experiencing it. Now I spend my days filling my heart with smile after smile, not letting anything get me down.

A lot of that space in my heart is filled by the opportunity to work with the children in the community. You watch them, and it breaks your heart to see how they try to navigate through really tough issues that burden them.

The tough part is when they have to do it alone. I feel an obligation to be there because if I am with them, I know I can make a difference for at least one of them.

I grew up in the same place that they did, and usually, within a couple of minutes, I can have their attention because a part of them was excited that someone from where they live made it.

A local person survived and became someone positive. A couple of minutes after explaining that, I have them believing that they can make it.

Seeing the overwhelming need for mentors helped me build the foundations for Dream 68 Inc. Right after my overdose, I signed up for Big Brothers Big Sisters. This effort gave me the spiritual lift I needed and the crucial support that the children were missing out on.

I had taken on a kid that was wanted by both the coaches and the gangsters. They pressured him to work on the streets for ugly wealth. He was big, brave, and strong. I worked really hard to help him understand mistakes that I made growing up and how I was there to support him while he worked through some of those difficult life choices the same way that some friend, some coach, or some teacher was there for me when I needed that support the most.

This first experience working with the youth has blossomed into more than I could have imagined. I have regularly scheduled programming for the community through motivational talks, support in the children's homeless shelters, and preparing future mentors.

I see myself in the position to have a positive influence on these kids. I learned quickly that when dealing with these underprivileged kids, know that they can sniff BS right away. You have to earn their trust.

They have to actually see that you are there to help them and not hurt them. I'm not going anywhere and am blessed to be able to help where I can.

Philanthropy comes with a great responsibility as well. There is nothing easy about giving back. It takes time, discipline, and thick skin to make a difference over a long period of time. If your passion is genuine, all the work you put into the organization will always pay off. It is all worth it if you think you can save even one life. Make a positive difference in just one person.

It is one of the most fulfilling experiences for me. It has given me a purpose after my playing days and even as I am growing older.

I have found a path and direction in life that involves an opportunity to heal while giving back. It is a huge blessing for me and my family. Beyond that, it has saved my life.

Every person I can help is a thanks to all the coaches, mentors, and family members that have helped me along the way. So from the bottom of my heart, to all those helping others and those who helped me, thank you.

Today

EPILOGUE BY DAVID LIONHEART

This book was inspired by an incredible journey that Gary took to Wisconsin twenty-one years after winning a championship with Green Bay. There were so many obstacles, emotions, and victories during those three days, so much so that it turned me into an author.

I started writing about the experience, and when I shared it with Gary, he told me to keep writing. So that became the book you just finished. We thought it would be important to include it in the book since it shows what a current weekend is like for Gary.

We take for granted little details in our lives that one day may become very challenging, like something as simple as turning the page to this book, having your vision to see the words, or having your hearing to listen to the manuscript being read aloud. Life is delicate and amazing both at the same time. We are learning to celebrate every day no matter what the circumstances. It takes work and time, but it's an investment you will never regret.

Enjoy the story that inspired me to write about this amazing man. You will not regret it, I promise.

Part 1: A New York Morning

Friday, 5:00 a.m. EST

The sun emitted a mixture of purples and blues to push away the spent evening sky. As my taxi driver willed his rattling sedan from Brooklyn to LaGuardia, the rays of light became so bright we could hardly make out the roads that we were jostling through. I closed my eyes and hoped he could see better than I could. This was a reminder that the day was here, was going to be long and was going to be one to remember. This was also a reminder to not waver in faith when the path is not clear. What this day will be remembered for was soon to be discovered.

I arrived an hour early to off-load my luggage, locate our gate, and score a wheelchair for Gary. It was our first time flying together, and we were embarking on an amazing trip to Milwaukee. This would be Gary's first time in twenty-one years going back to Wisconsin—a place where he created some of his most memorable relationships with his friends, Green Bay, and the game of football. Along the way, he also created a formula that would define him as a young man: screenshots of life experiences that he could look back on now to reflect on and learn from. This trip would become the catalyst for a storm of heavy emotions both good and bad.

I watched Gary slowly emerge from the car on this early New York morning and, as always, with a smile. I have known him long enough now to tell when the smile is forced. I can tell when the conditions are tough on him and when the pain is very present from his injuries. Like I said, though, he always has a smile on.

We were ushered through security and found ourselves in the terminal where we would wait for the plane. I shared a fishing magazine that my son picked for "Mr. Brown because he likes fishies." My four-year-old has grown up knowing Gary and is not intimidated by his size and color like I might have been growing up. I always use descriptors like *fisherman, tall, strong,* and *happy* when talking about Gary with my son.

Gary is a handsomely dark, large-framed man with broad shoulders and an unassuming size when sitting. When he stands up, he is like Optimus Prime transforming from a truck to a superhero. His hands will instantly consume yours during a friendly shake, and his heart will fully care for you within the first few minutes of knowing him. As he speaks, your ears receive genuine consoling words from this gentle giant.

After Gary was drafted by the Steelers in '94, he was pulled off the waiver wire by Green Bay. Gary had no idea where Green Bay even was. He gathered his things and traveled out there. He arrived at the airport where he was one of the few people, if not the only person, not White.

He would come to learn that a large dark man in Green Bay was likely heading to the stadium to play football. He arrived in a small hotel where he would remain until his lodging situation with his new team was finalized. He called up his mother immediately upon arrival, describing a few of the places he could see from the hotel room window in case he went missing. He half-jokingly and half-seriously said this so that she would have a lead to give the authorities if he went missing.

We chuckle at this moment, but in the early '90s, closed-minded racism was still very present in our society and presented real issues for people with dark skin. Gary often speaks on these situations during games, commenting on the horrific slurs that were hurled at him and his teammates when they were on the road. He says they had a mentality of staying focused on the game and doing their job. Those people were not going to break their spirit no matter how vulgar they were.

Gary would go on to discover that Green Bay was the NFL's best-kept secret. The love from the community was never ending. This love would become very important during some tough times Gary would experience as he was adjusting as a young man in a large spotlight.

Back in the terminal, we both handled some last-minute business over a steaming cup of overpriced coffee. Our breakfast was being chased by words of logistical confirmations surrounding our adventure.

Gary was going to do his first autograph signing in Wisconsin in over twenty years. Understanding the gravity of this situation, I had to tag along to witness it firsthand. As a bonus, I scheduled a visit to the Milwaukee VA. We have a policy to always be ourselves and to help anyone we come across that needs it no matter where we are or what we are doing.

Gary and I met through one of our team members and have been working together within the veteran community since January 28, 2016. He has been to almost all of our workshops over the past three and a half years, so this was no different.

We play football with veterans every month in New York and New Jersey among a range of satellite programs all over the country. The football community is very New York Giants/Jets faithful. However, once these raging fans meet Gary Brown of the Green Bay Packers, they find he has won over their hearts because of the man he is.

This trip was heading back to a place where Gary was still known even after twenty years of being away. The love that he would encounter would be his to lose. However, he was coming back as a different person. He has made changes in his life and mindset that have been putting him on this new path. This new journey was one that was focused on living a long, happy life, not living for the quick, hollow thrills.

It is a very polarizing change to be living as a celebrity, submerged in the party lifestyle, and playing on the largest stage in the world and then returning to a "regular" life. Gary found himself working at least four jobs in the fields of management, construction, maintenance, and security. He felt the need to uphold that status and the cost of walking into a bar and having everyone spit your name, hoping for a free drink. It's almost like asking for a false sense of appreciation without knowing it and working twice as hard to get it.

You have to find your thrills in other ways that will not slowly kill you over time. Gary was beginning to rediscover the value in giving back to yourself, giving back to your community, and most difficult of all, a new career after football. This journey was in the hopes of helping him answer some of those questions, and maybe after all this time, there was still a life for Gary in his "home away from home."

Part 2: All Aboard

The muffled flight announcement filled the crowded gate area, prompting us to board first. Gary was pushed in the shiny red commercial-grade wheelchair to the open door of the plane at the bottom of the Jetway.

That in itself takes a lot of bravery, to which I give Gary and his new mindset a lot of credit. Of course, he would prefer to walk proudly into the airport on his own two feet, wielding a large mine of gold sprinkled with timeless diamonds in the notorious shape of the Green Bay Packers *G* on his treelike ring finger. That wasn't the case. Today he proudly sat, knowing that his spiritual journey was in full speed. He remained steadfast in not caring what people thought from the book cover but relishing in what people thought about him once they opened up his book.

I began to sense an uneasy aura about him. It was almost like if the wheelchair had a reverse button on it, he might have considered pushing it. Alas, with no reverse button, we came to a creeping halt at the plane door. The assistant locked the rusty brake on the chair as if it were an open-air jail cell.

Inside was a smiling and sweet woman who greeted us. Waving, she invited our gentle giant and myself into the tiny model-like plane. Gary crouched down to swing his head into the jet. His cane should have been a lit torch helping guide him down the dark plastic tunnel—the one leading to our closely bolted-down seats.

Gary was mumbling some nervous words of concern regarding his size and the size of the plane as we slowly crept to the seats labeled 8C and 8D. I slid into the window seat so he could have the aisle. He was hesitant to get in. Seeing this, a nearby flight attendant heading home after a long shift offered Gary her seat in the exit row. He declined because he preferred to sit next to me but gratefully left it an open-ended game-time decision.

Gary finally joined me in the compact seating arrangement; we were like two peas in a pod. The air had not been turned on yet, and he was feeling it. It was as if we were consuming the final exhale of relief from the hundred passengers who just landed.

He looked at me after less than a minute of sitting down and bluntly told me, "I can't do this, and I need to get off the plane. I'm very claustrophobic." Without hesitation, I supported the decision, and we traced our steps back to the outside of the plane door. One by one, the other passengers curiously walked by us to board the plane as Gary and I talked through the situation.

His mindset was to rent a car and drive to Milwaukee or wait for a bigger plane. I thought that was fair and totally understandable. Flying sucks and is scary on its own, and then when you mix internal emotion and an uncontrollable fear, the dread alone propels you to the nearest Hertz desk, securing any other mode of transportation.

We had already checked his walker and all our bags and sports equipment for the VA fitness workshop. I had to make the call to leave Gary and continue to Milwaukee, which was not an easy decision. I simply told him that on the other side of that plane ride were sixty vets waiting for us. They would be anxiously waiting for us to arrive and play football with them.

They, of course, couldn't care less about me and really would want him, but I would find a way to smooth the situation over. Gary has a reputation of showing up even on his worst days. He can be a hot mess and yet finds the strength to show up to our appointments. At our workshops, we are not just playing football; we are delivering hope to people who need it. Gary uses that as motivation to make sure he shows up. He always says, "I can suffer at home alone, or I can suffer here with you all."

After I explained this to Gary, he started cooking in the kitchen between his ears. I knew in his heart he did not want this to be the way it went. I offered hope that perhaps the AC was on now and how it might feel better to board. We were definitely the last ones on because the smiling flight attendant was waiting for us to make the call.

Gary flicked the switch and willingly walked back into the tin cave. Thank God I felt a wave of cool air greet us before the rows of curious faces. We had to walk the tightrope of confusion as we made our way back into the seats. Gary fixed his earbuds, pumped some relaxing music, and texted his girl that it was not going to be easy but that he was going to try and fly.

I opened my book and looked down while keeping a third eye on every movement he was making, monitoring his vitals like I had x-ray vision. I stared into the book blankly, thinking, *Holy shit, that just happened, and it's not nearly over yet.* I was so proud of him for having the courage to at least try again. Being calm was very important for both of us. Composure and smooth decision-making are contagious. Gary needed to do that for himself even though he was going through hell on the inside. He wanted nothing more than getting off that plane. Despite the tides being against us, off we went.

If you are able-bodied and unaware, you probably take things for granted all day long, little things like getting up and going to the restroom. On a trip of his to the bathroom during the flight, I watched him having to walk in the space sideways to fit his head into the upper angle of the chemically scented nook. We both knew that if the door closed behind him, he might not be able to get it back open again.

I think he was composed of more volume than the micropotty this plane had to offer. The plane started to rock with turbulence, and Gary still managed to make it out and back to our home base with an uneasy chuckle.

This might seem like a strange detail, but it was a small victory to add to his commitment to flying that day. He was already in a vulnerable state where the slightest offset could crumble him. He became comfortable in his decision and started to own it. He not only flew on the plane but existed on it.

Part 3: Touchdown

Friday, 10:17 a.m. CST

After two and a half hours of slow, high-elevated torture, the sound of the runway hitting our rubberized points of contact echoed in the cabin. We made it.

With a hurried pace, we gathered our luggage and game equipment so we could catch the shuttle. Without stopping to think, we were delivered to the hotel to drop off our belongings, get changed into our fitness gear, and climb back into the Uber. His arrival would spark the first interest among the locals that a Super Bowl champion was staying in the hotel. We would learn as the trip went on that this intel would spread like wildfire.

Gary was a trooper during this fast-paced travel. It takes him great effort to walk and get around. What you may not know is that at one time, his doctors told him he would not walk again. He was paralyzed from the waist down. He had to adjust to this as part of his life after football. A man who always earned everything that he ever had with his hands and his feet was now bed- and chair-ridden.

This would foster some of the darkest moments in his life as he was figuring out what the disabled life was going to be like. Living back home after a star-studded career and Super Bowl championship, he found himself in a paralyzed pity party and rightfully so.

I recall Gary telling me that at one point in time, he dropped some ash off the end of his cigar and did not realize it burned through his pants. It was slowly burning through the skin on his leg, and that's when he smelled the flesh cooking. Situations like this left him stuck in a place of depression and helplessness.

His pride was shrinking smaller and smaller with every detail that surfaced that involved losing his independence and former identity. He found himself in such a sorry rhythm of slamming down a fistful of medication and pain killers, so much so that at one point during his recovery, he accidentally overdosed.

Luckily, a call to 911 saved him that morning, but he had an even bigger call to make: a call to himself. He started to realize the alcohol and drugs were keeping him blind from a life he could be living. He lifted the most important weight you can lift off yourself: the weight that makes you feel sorry for yourself. It's the weight that stops you from realizing that no matter how bad your situation is, there are others out there that are going through much worse. Those are the ones that need our help.

Friday, 1:17 p.m. CST

These travel details may sound simple and uneventful for an able-bodied person, but what has happened to Gary in the last five hours was like doing an Ironman competition. He made it this far, and we were in a speeding Uber, approximately thirty minutes away from stepping foot onto the campus of the Milwaukee VA.

The driver had no idea that he was transporting a wave of energy that had started after Gary's overdose. Gary was inspired by a quadriplegic he saw on TV one night. He was a man with no arms and legs telling able-bodied people how to live a healthy and happy life. He was confused and blown away. Most importantly, he was inspired. He started to soul-search and realized that if he didn't get out of the house no matter what his condition was, he would not be able to go on.

He began his philanthropic mission at this time. During his career, he thought about volunteering, but it did not fit in the schedule. The sports, parties, and every other excuse not to do it lay in the path. Now, with a fresh mindset and appreciation for life, Gary was ready to take on what would be his second championship run.

He volunteered with Big Brothers Big Sisters, and it changed his life. He set aside his problems to help local youth overcome the overwhelming adversity that faces them, especially in a low-income setting. He didn't know it yet, but he was about to change the lives of so many children, homeless community members, and transitioning veterans.

It was this new mindset that Gary had that brought him to Play for Your Freedom on January 28, 2016. He decided he was going to help anyone who needed it and that if he couldn't do it himself, he would find someone who could. Gary came out on that day with his fellow alumni and helped coach veterans in a PTSD unit.

The veterans showed up in a negative mindset because they really didn't know where they were going. The tides would quickly change. Football became the tool to help these men and women overcome their overwhelming problems of the moment. Gary and our team watched twenty-six faces walk in with flat expressions and then leave the football field sweaty and smiling.

Now, three and a half years later, we were in a car filled with footballs and cones, heading to a VA hospital near where Gary spent his NFL career. I was lucky enough to be a part of this journey and observe the powerful moments and surprises that were happening.

We, of course, arrived on time at the quiet, well-groomed campus and, like clockwork, got into game-day mode. We were greeted by an incredible whole-health staff who would contribute so much positive energy to this very special day.

We have done this over a hundred times now, and still, there is a lingering wrench in our guts. He and I never outwardly say it to one another, but it's there and weighs heavy. We really want to make a positive impact. You always hope you are well received by the group you are meeting. We made a commitment to each other to always be ourselves when we work on our projects. This is important because if you are yourself, your intentions will be clear to those you are seeking to help.

A bad day for our team is when someone who has played football with us ends up taking their own life. It is the ultimate pain, one that cannot be reversed. The severity of it is so powerful that it has to be one of the factors that pushed Gary to get back on that plane to get here. It was a matter of life and death, not our own death but those who we might not be able to reach.

Anyone can extend a friendly gesture, but what we want to accomplish is to help these veterans flick a switch to go from dark to light. It doesn't always happen at first, but if you keep your course and that mission in mind, then there is a good chance you will get there. If we can help just one person, it is worth all the sacrifices along the way.

Part 4: Talk the Talk

Friday, 2:02 p.m. CST

As we approached the stark facility, one young lady wearing a football jersey was right at the door. By the end of the event, she would go on to stand out in my mind as an all-star. She was a veteran and a *huge* football fan. But she was not just any fan; she was a Green Bay fan. I had not understood the gravity of the fanfare until I walked off the plane and found myself surrounded by foam cheese hats and footballs as far as the eye could see. I understood it even more when I met this young lady.

These fans are not new or accidental. They are born, they are faithful, and they have been rooted in the game since the very beginning of the National Football League.

I began setting up the fields for play, educating the staff on procedures, and enjoying the sunshine. We made it here, and that was our main competition so far. Gary sat under a shady tree, small-talking with some obvious fans who worked at the VA. One by one, the veterans started filling empty grassy areas.

Men, women, and service dogs circled the prepped outdoor arena, anticipating the workshop. They came to meet the advertised Super Bowl champion from the Packers, but there was going to be a stronger bond forged today than a fan experience. Gary was going to include these war heroes in his journey and his current state of mind—one we can all benefit from understanding.

It was time to break the silence. I spoke first and started by educating everyone on our program. I was feeding off the energy of the attentive audience. I always thank everyone for having the courage to leave their rooms and come out for the workshop. This is the first step to allowing yourself the opportunity to socialize and heal.

I always emphasize that it's okay to hurt and that no one is cast aside for any reason at our workshops. Everyone has a place and purpose no matter what their age or ability. We operate in a judgement-free zone. All of us have a story to tell, and most importantly, there are very deep wounds that outsiders and even close friends cannot see. We use this space to help those wounds heal through fellowship and fitness.

I gripped a matte black helmet with a lion on it. The philosophy behind this helmet that we were gifting to the veterans at this VA was an important one: although we have been through hell, we can carry our scars proudly. Most importantly, we can be made beautiful again and find our purpose. That was the cement that had been poured into Gary's new foundations.

I knew that the crowd appreciated what I had to say but could not wait to hear Gary speak. I have heard Gary speak on so many occasions in so many different environments and to so many diverse audiences. He never preplans his talk. There are always new nuggets of knowledge, old stories, and words of hope that make a fresh appearance.

I turned the mic over to Gary and joined the tightly gathered crowd. We could not see his eyes through the tinted sunglasses resting on his nose. He sat with his hands woven into each other, resting his arms on the sides of his walker. It hit him. At that moment, it became a reality that he was actually back in Wisconsin for the first time in twenty-one years. As he uttered those words to the crowd, they gave him a welcoming round of applause.

This was a powerful moment because in the military community, being welcomed home is such a huge part of their transition. It is what you yearn for while you are away right up to the moment your tattered boots are back on American soil. Receiving this kind of love from this exceptional group of warriors would be with Gary for the rest of his life.

He was able to ground himself and start his talk from his roots in Long Island. It was as if Gary was composing the perfect symphony of details, talking through some of the toughest times of his life like the humiliating moments during his paralysis where nurses had to fully care for him and dark moments where he found himself at the bottom of a bottle—all the information a fan would never get to hear about their heralded gladiators of Green Bay. Not only were they getting to learn about him, but it was coming from his heart. And there were only a few feet of empty grass separating everyone.

Word by word, Gary explained how he found himself through this journey right down to the moment of being there in that field. The audience was silent. Tears slowly fell from behind sets of stoic sunglasses and rolled slowly down the cheeks of the listeners. Something very special was happening here. Gary was not just preaching his advice. He was living it.

The connection between them was found in a space where it was okay to ask for help. It is not easy to become a new person when you so deeply want to remain the person you once knew and identified with. It is possible to transition to a new person when you dedicate yourself to give back to others.

It is possible when you start to respect yourself and embrace the person you are now. This message was being delivered to the adult audience this afternoon, but Gary spends a lot of his time focusing on delivering that message to the children in his community.

Gary understands how crucial it is that our youth are empowered and educated on these life lessons. He dedicates countless hours doing so in his "men into mentors" programming he has created. He comes from a strong household with incredible parents and siblings. This structure has always been a safe place for Gary.

Just the same, he knows a lot of kids do not have that structure. He seeks out those voids and strives to fill them in. He puts himself into place to give support to the children who might feel like the streets are their only way to succeed.

Gary gives them a visual and voice that a kid from Brentwood can become a superstar and fulfill their dreams. Equally as important, they can navigate through life's hardships if they are willing to ask for help from positive people around them.

Gary and I work well together on the speaking platform, and I always know when to come in to close the ceremony. The crowd was so appreciative of his vulnerability and showed it with genuine emotion, projecting love his way with cheers, handshakes, and hugs.

From that moment on, the energy was full speed ahead. We kept it going and moved everyone on to the next phase of this journey. Let the games begin! The sun was shining a little differently today. I watched in silence as the groups of veterans smiled and caught passes. It was almost as if it moved in slow motion because nobody out there wanted it to end.

Friday, 4:47 p.m.

We played until we could not play anymore. Now we were spent. We started to feel the fatigue from the wave of emotions getting here, the messages delivered, and all the football we played. We did it, and nothing got in our way. Nothing ever does. We needed to rest.

There was a sigh of relief on the ride home. We didn't have to take an hour-long Uber ride with a stranger as we did to get there because the rec coordinator drove us back to our hotel, and we were so thankful. We looked at each other with a slight smile, knowing that we did it.

Upon returning, we tried to slink through the hotel lobby and catch the next elevator up. We were greeted by the staff all huddled around the front desk. The maintenance team must have been mopping the lobby for hours, waiting for Gary to get here.

You cannot get Gary through a room or out of an event. It's a journey filled with people wanting one more moment, one more story, and of course, one more picture together. He's so humble, and he genuinely loves it.

By now, we were running on fumes. In typical fashion, he sucked it up and cracked that contagious smile, and off went the camera flashes. I unloaded the sharpies and photos onto the desk, and we began working the room. Once everyone had a photo for themselves, their families and friends were graciously asked to catch up with everyone later on. I felt like we couldn't get up to our rooms fast enough.

We agreed to meet up for dinner later on that night but both needed some downtime to exhale. I wondered what he was doing once he got into his room. The journey he just experienced was so intense from the moment he slowly crept out of his car at five o'clock this morning until now.

I was relieved that we completed everything needed on the workshop side. We touched the lives of many people today in such a positive way. I was thankful Gary made it through healthy and made it all happen safely. I wondered what he was thinking about and then thought, *Hopefully nothing.* He needed to rest his mind and heal. He embarked on something so new and so special today. That takes time to process, I would imagine, and we didn't have much time. We had to recharge because tomorrow's signing would prove to be just as intense.

Part 5: This Belongs to You

Saturday, 12:23 p.m. CST

As we made our way into the echoing gymnasium of the Salvation Army Community Center, we navigated through seemingly endless rows of folding tables covered in perfectly placed old and grayed collecting cards. Each collector was equally proud of the variety and players they had for sale.

Rectangles of passion were wrapped in hard plastic cases stacked on top of each other. Packed on every precise four-cornered tablet were statistics, photos of the good old days, and history itself.

As Gary slowly made his way to the back corner of the gymnasium, we saw the area sectioned off for what would host today's alumni Super Bowl champions signing. Gary made himself comfortable for what was thought to be a place to meet fans. It would become much more than that.

As the day progressed, it turned into the location where Gary would receive positive nostalgia, appreciation, and love. Gary was teamed up with two other champs: one who played with him and another incredible young man who won a Super Bowl some years after him. Although there was an age gap, that same Packer pride remains in every one of the athletes that comes through Green Bay.

Sometimes called the NFL's best-kept secret, these players have countless stories on and off the field from their time in that culture. These form the possibility of having a great career and a connection with the world's greatest fan base. There are generations of men, women, and children that follow and adore these sports heroes. They appreciate the players for what they do for their community and for their football team.

We met a young man who actually shipped me his football with almost every player from the championship team's signature on it to New York. He asked me to have Gary sign it, thinking he would never ever get to meet him. We did just that, and yet here they were years later, face-to-face. It was surreal in a way but kept pace with the theme of this trip.

The topic of Gary's distance from Green Bay seemed to come up often during the signing. This played a part in the emotional journey that Gary was making back here to connect with his fans and himself. This young man was not the only one who attended that day in surprise, excitement, and anticipation.

One by one, fans carrying photos of Gary, Super Bowl patches, framed artwork, garments, and rare books cycled through the table like a factory assembly line. Many times the families uttered, "You're the last one I needed on this football" and "You're the missing player on this team roster poster." These people were completing priceless collections of sports memorabilia almost as if they were clicking in the last piece of a daunting puzzle.

On the other side of the table, I watched Gary become consumed with love, admiration, and affection from these families. There were small children giggling while they tried on his Super

Bowl ring. Fans who faithfully cheered him on every Sunday were now placing their hands inside his massive grip for a true sign of respect and genuine pride.

Every piece of affection was delicately placed on that big man's heart, emotional pieces of patchwork restoring something within him he did not know was hurt so badly. He was experiencing feelings he never knew could feel so good upon coming home to Wisconsin.

A smiling man proudly walked up to the table, bearing a distinct yellow game helmet. I saw a look on Gary's face develop. He immediately looked under the sweat-soaked chin strap. There was a faded inscription noting number 71. Without question, Gary knew this was the piece of armor he placed on his head before all his games, including the Super Bowl victory.

Gary pointed excitedly to the battle scars etched into the hard plastic yellow dome. Coincidentally, we had a photo of Gary on the table that had enough detail to match his claims. It was awesome to see, but now we had to get back to business. The man asked him to sign the helmet with his name and the inscription "Game-worn."

The signing seemed to last for an eternity. Gary kept on spinning the helmet as if it was sitting on a lazy Susan. His eyes scanned over every detail, soaking it up for all he could. Then almost reluctantly, he reached out and pushed the helmet back to its owner. It reminded me of a child who was given five minutes to play with a toy and, when the timer had gone off, had to give it back to their sibling.

The man had numerous items to be signed and was clearly a first-class fan. After double-checking all the transactions, he gathered his belongings and walked away just like that.

The fans continued to roll through the bustling sports event one after the other over the next hour. Surprisingly, we noticed a familiar face return to the front of the line. Even the current customers were confused.

He came back, bearing the war-torn skull piece of a professional football player. With the perfect mixture of confidence and conviction, he placed it on the table where he had once accepted it.

It was as if an ocean wind had shifted as he sincerely pushed the helmet back toward Gary. It gracefully landed into his large, firm grip. Gary cradled it as if he was holding a delicate newborn baby in his hands.

Gary slowly raised his head with a look of surprise and wonder on his face, silently asking what was next.

"This belongs to you."

We were all in disbelief that the man just gifted it back. Everyone standing around that table knew this was an irreplaceable piece of equipment that would be so important to any player reconnecting with it. The gentleman selflessly gave it up, knowing it meant more to Gary than sitting on his own shelf.

You see, a lot of fans came to take that day, but the genuine kindness of that man would stand out. He had forged a bond with one of his favorite football players, and that is something that Gary will never forget. I know for sure this helmet will sit among other trophies, awards, and photos, but it will shine among the rest. It became a spiritual currency for both people. Now it was back to business as the show went on.

Gary and the other players facilitated a very special connection with the fans while carefully signing items of their playing history and sharing pearls of knowledge with the children that came through the lines, humanizing themselves as athletes and explaining that the road is not always easy. He directly connected with the kids and emphasized that no matter how hard it was, they should follow their dreams and stay focused.

These men each had a large studded ring on their hands, designating them champions forever in Green Bay's history books, but we cannot forget that they are people too. They are people who worked really hard to get to that point.

To play at a championship level and become the best in the world is such a huge accolade for any athlete. During the preparation to play at that level for that long, they also had to juggle the life that came with it. Countless struggles and adversities fill the moments in their lives that the fans do not get to see.

The sum of it all is that life goes on. Those dark moments of struggle become valuable pieces of knowledge and reflection.

Experiences evolve over time and become even brighter than the heavy gold ring that sits on their fingers.

I learned so much about the broader life of an athlete at this event, especially how balance is so important for everyone. And with the right balance within their complicated lives, champions can remain champions forever.

Part 6: Finish What We Started

Sunday, 5:17 a.m. CST

I was on a separate flight from Gary coming home, which, at the time of booking the flight, didn't seem like that big of a deal. However, I was a little nervous about this flight when the journey began to unfold and we had not even arrived in Wisconsin yet. After watching Gary own moment after moment during this trip, I was no longer concerned about him getting back.

While meditating and doing my morning push-ups in a quiet corner of the terminal, I saw a call coming in from Gary. His flight was not until noon, so this worried me a little. He expressed how special this weekend was for him in so many words and thanked me for being a part of it. Admittedly, I was the thankful one.

It is not often you can sit in the front seat of such an incredible journey. It was the next step in his path and our destiny. It has been continuously built for five years now. We met in the arena of community service. The game changed when we realized we could help heal ourselves at the same time. Asking for help is okay, but sometimes it's a hard thing to do.

You think he was holding up his Super Bowl trophy, thinking, *I better enjoy this because I'm going to be paralyzed in a couple of years?* Of course, not! When the injury happened, he had to tap back into that inner champion—that inner strength. It's the kind of strength you cannot see; you can only witness it in one's actions.

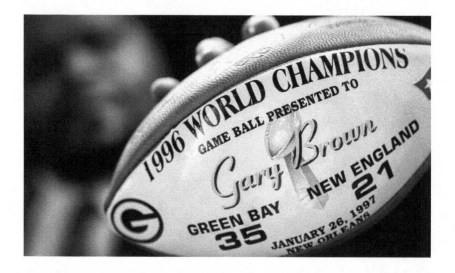

I sat and watched Gary heal his soul while making his story available to others who may really need to hear it so they know that someone else is always fighting much more than we are and that they are not alone if something troubles them. Daily battles can lead up to daily victories if we are willing to fight them. I witnessed it firsthand on this trip.

We left Wisconsin having experienced what would be a pivotal moment in Gary's life. The journey provided proof he was still very loved by the community and fan base in Wisconsin.

When the time came for his flight, I closed my eyes and pictured Gary filled with love in his heart, proudly walking into his plane home, gingerly squeezing into his seat next to a stranger who would have no idea where Gary just came from, putting on his headphones one at a time, and smiling nervously, excited to be heading back to New York.

This experience was not given to him. He had to earn it literally every step of the way.

I'm assuming the flight took off

Gary Brown

Not yet lol, they better hurry or they will be 350 pounds lighter

Lol, Close your eyes and think about all the good that came of you getting on that first plane. You got this

Gary Brown

Thanks guys, see you on the other side

About the Author

Gary Lee Brown is a proud Long Island native. He graduated from Brentwood High School in 1989, earning his high school diploma. Following high school, Gary continued his passion of playing football and attended Nassau Community College.

After graduating from Nassau Community College, Gary received an athletic scholarship to the prestigious Georgia School of Technology (Georgia Tech) in 1992.

While pursuing his degree at Georgia Tech, Gary's outstanding performance on the football field was observed by the National Football League. In 1994, Gary was drafted in the fifth round by the Pittsburgh Steelers and was acquired by the Green Bay Packers later that year.

While with the Green Bay Packers, Gary's contribution and dedication assisted the Packers in winning the Super Bowl in 1997. After ending his tenure with the Green Bay Packers, Gary then played for a variety of teams domestically and internationally.

It was after football that Gary faced some of his greatest challenges both physically and mentally. Finding himself paralyzed from the waist down after a work incident, Gary fell into a deep and dark place of depression. He then chose to help heal others in order to help heal himself.

Throughout Gary's life journey, he remained steadfast on the principles and morals instilled in him by his loving parents, Bettie Brown and Tommie Brown. These attributes continue to reward our community as Gary is actively giving back as a mentor to at-youth risk and is available for the enhancement of any societal needs.

CPSIA information can be obtained
at www.ICGtesting.com
Printed in the USA
JSHW011457091122
32828JS00003B/11